# Scriptural & Topical Indices to LBW

Paul E. Schuessler, Thomas R. Bartsch, David P. Rebeck

**C.S.S. Publishing Company, Inc.**
Lima, Ohio

SCRIPTURAL AND TOPICAL INDICES TO LBW

Copyright © 1985 by
The C.S.S. Publishing Company, Inc.
Lima, Ohio

All rights reserved. No portion of this book may be reproduced or utilized in any form or by any means, electronic or mechanical including photocopying, without permission in writing from the publisher. Inquiries should be addressed to: The C.S.S. Publishing Company, Inc., 628 South Main Street, Lima, Ohio 45804.

This book is based in part on material first published in *Lutheran Book of Worship* and *Lutheran Book of Worship: Minister's Desk Edition*, copyright © 1978 by Lutheran Church in America, The American Lutheran Church, The Evangelical Lutheran Church of Canada, and The Lutheran Church — Missouri Synod. "Topical References," "Hymns for the Church Year," and "Scriptural References in Hymns" are adapted and revised by permission of Augsburg Publishing House.

5811/ISBN 0-89536-727-0                                    PRINTED IN U.S.A.

## How I Use These Indices

A few years ago, some figures circulated which indicated that the average Lutheran congregation uses only about 50 to 75 different hymns in the course of the church year. Allowing for a certain number of seasonal hymns, i.e. Advent/Christmas, Lent/Easter, this indicated that many congregations will repeat a relatively small number of hymns with great frequency. While there is something to be said for selecting familiar hymns that everyone can sing, this practice allows many hymns to fall into disuse which in turn tends to make their selection in the future all the more unlikely.

Beyond the responsibility of church musicians to keep the wealth of Lutheran hymnody alive, creative hymn selection can greatly enhance the worship service. It is our hope that this volume will facilitate such creative hymn selection. Whether the task of selecting hymns is assigned to the pastor and/or organist, or a worship committee, this volume should make the task less intimidating and a lot more enjoyable, both in the actual selection process and in the final result — the singing of hymns in the worship service.

A few observations that have proved helpful to us:

1. First, decide on the readings and psalmody for the day, either using the lectionary or another source, and also have the sermon themes prepared in advance.

2. Allow plenty of time to select hymns. I find that it usually takes about a half hour per Sunday. Also, the process seems to lend itself to working on more than one Sunday at a sitting. I generally pick hymns for at least a month at a time, often times for a whole season of the church year.

3. Generally, I tend to refer to the Scriptural References first, using the assigned readings for the day and checking to see what hymns are available on a particular text. Then, if hymns remain to be selected, I refer to the Topical References, with the general themes of the readings already in mind. The Topical References also tend to be used more extensively during the festival half of the church year when themes are more immediately apparent.

4. Keep a frequency chart. This can be done by simply marking the date at the top of each page in a specially reserved hymnal. Then, once every year or so, page through this hymnal, listing those hymns which have not been selected in a while. This list can then be used in conjunction with these indices for future hymn selection.

Careful hymn selection can be a time-consuming process, but the end result is well worth the effort. It can enhance the readings for the day, underscore the theme of the service, and focus the worship service for the congregation and worship leaders. Obviously, each congregation has differing traditions and favorite hymns; but with care, these traditions can be continually expanded, shedding new light on the words of the psalmist, "Sing to the Lord a *new* song."

Thomas R. Bartsch
21 December, 1984
The Feast of St. Thomas, Apostle

## Introduction

Important as it is, selecting hymns can be a real chore. There is a German proverb to that effect: *Liederauswahl ist Lieder Qual* (Picking hymns is painful). It need not be.

For the most part, this resource will enable the hymn selector to avoid inadvertantly dropping a choice hymn.

Musically, it will help the organist, if she or he is the one who selects hymns. Let us say the pastor provides the organist with the text and theme of the day. The organist will then be able to look at a number of options. Not every hymn can be used as a processional hymn.

These indices will make it easier to more quickly find a hymn to match I) any of the major texts of Scripture or II) a topic or an occasion.

Careful selecting of hymns better adapts *The Lutheran Book of Worship* to the experience, taste, and growth potential of a congregation in hymnody. The indices will help focus and coordinate the theme of a worship service, making it more meaningful and inspiring.

Preachers, teachers and writers will find these indices valuable in locating quotations for sermons, lectures, and devotional materials.

I. Scriptural References, page 9, doubles the number listed in Scriptural References in Hymns, page 468ff of the *Ministers Desk Edition of the Lutheran Book of Worship*. II. Topical References, page 57, doubles the number listed in Topical Index of Hymns, page 932ff of the *The Lutheran Book of Worship*.

*Scriptural Indices to The Lutheran Book of Worship* may also be used with a concordance to *The Lutheran Book of Worship*, which at this writing has been proposed for publication by Augsburg and Fortress. They supplement one another.

> Let the word of Christ dwell in you richly as you teach and admonish one another in all wisdom, and as you sing psalms and hymns and spiritual songs with thankfulness in your hearts to God.
>
> Colossians 3:16

Gathering references like this has been a complex and difficult task. Some of the selections have been, of necessity, subjective. Where slips or errors are detected, we ask your understanding and help. Please forward suggestions to the publishers. The enlarged use of hymnody is the work of the whole church. It is a growing experience we would like to share in future editions.

                        Laus Deo!

                        Paul E. Schuessler
                        Thomas R. Bartsch
                        David P. Rebeck
                        A.D. 1984

## Preface

"Sing unto the Lord a new song, sing unto the Lord all the earth."

One of the treasures of the Lutheran heritage has been congregational singing of hymns. Martin Luther said that, "Music is a beautiful and glorious gift of God and close to theology."

But music is not an end in itself. It was intended to be used in the service of God's Word, to enhance and illuminate the text of Scripture. The melody of the hymn serves as a commentary on the text, making music itself exegesis.

This set of indices will assist worship planners to select hymns which are appropriate to the Lessons and theme of the day. Although *The Lutheran Book of Worship* contains such suggestions, it is not comprehensive, and hymns are not listed according to their underlying Scriptural text.

Frequently the biblical material is located in the middle verses and not in the title, and so may be overlooked by worship planners. This comprehensive set of indices is therefore a welcome addition to the set of companion volumes to *The Lutheran Book of Worship*. In this volume the hymns are related to the Scripture according to the sequence of biblical books, making possible a convenient correlation of text with hymn.

The editors are to be congratulated for their help in keeping our focus on God's Word expressed in music and word.

*Christ is the theme of our songs of praise and thus shall we indicate that we desire to sing and to tell that Christ alone is our Savior.*
— Martin Luther

Carl A. Volz
Luther Northwestern Seminary
Saint Paul, Minnesota

# I

## SCRIPTURE REFERENCES IN HYMNS

## GENESIS

| | | |
|---|---|---|
| 1:1 | **374** | We all believe in one true God |
| 1:1-2 | **413** | Father eternal, ruler of creation |
| 1:1-3 | **179 v2** | At the name of Jesus |
| 1:1-4 | **281** | God, who made the earth and heaven |
| | **400** | God, whose almighty word |
| 1:1-5 | **463** | God, who stretched the spangled heavens |
| 1:2 | **164** | Creator Spirit, by whose aid |
| | **467** | Eternal Father, strong to save |
| 1:26-31 | **463** | God, who stretched the spangled heavens |
| 1:3-5 | **233** | Thy strong word did cleave the darkness |
| | **521** | Let us with a gladsome mind |
| | **266** | Maker of the earth and heaven |
| Ch.3 | **372** | In Adam we have all been one |
| 3:1-15 | **153** | "Welcome, happy morning!" age to age shall say |
| 3:15 | **155** | Praise the Savior, now and ever |
| 4:1-16 | **372** | In Adam we have all been one |
| 4:10 | **95** | Glory be to Jesus |
| 5:22-24 | **270** | God of our life, all-glorious Lord |
| 11:1-9 | **413 v3** | Father eternal, ruler of creation |
| 11:9 | **54 v2** | It came upon the midnight clear |
| Chs. 12-25 | **544** | The God of Abraham praise |
| 18:27 | **438** | Lord, teach us how to pray aright |
| 22:16 | **544 v4** | The God of Abraham praise |
| 28:16-18 | **186** | How blessed is this place, O Lord |
| | **375** | Only-begotten, Word of God eternal |
| 28:20-22 | **477** | O God of Jacob, by whose hand |

## EXODUS

| | | |
|---|---|---|
| 3:6 | **544** | The God of Abraham praise |
| 3:14 | **544** | The God of Abraham praise |
| 10:11 | **389** | Stand up, stand up for Jesus |
| 12:22 | **141** | The day of resurrection! |
| | **210** | At the Lamb's high feast we sing |
| 12:22, 26-27 | **141** | The day of resurrection! |
| | **p. 144** | In the Service of Light (Evening Prayer) |
| 13:21 | **343** | Guide me ever, great Redeemer |
| 13:21-22 | **358** | Glories of your name are spoken |
| | **557** | Let all things now living |
| 14:22 | **210** | At the Lamb's high feast we sing |
| Ch. 15 | **p.148** | Canticle –19 I will sing to the Lord (Ministers Edition pp. 148, 465; Cantemus Domino) |

## EXODUS (continued)

| | | |
|---|---|---|
| 15:1-21 | **132** | Come, you faithful, raise the strain |
| 19:4 | **544 v4** | The God of Abraham praise |
| | **543 v2** | Praise to the Lord, the Almighty, the King of creation |
| 19:9-13 | **34** | O come, oh, come, Emmanuel |
| 23:16ff | **404** | As saints of old their first fruits brought |
| 23:19 | **410** | We give thee but thine own |
| 25:19 | **524** | My God, how wonderful thou art |
| 33:17-23 | **327** | Rock of Ages, cleft for me |
| 33:20 | **165 v3** | Holy, holy, holy, Lord God Almighty! |

## NUMBERS

| | | |
|---|---|---|
| 6 | **P. 74, 95, 117** | The Benediction in the Orders for Holy Communion |
| | **247** | Holy Majesty, before you |
| | **440** | Christians, while on earth abiding |
| | **259** | Lord, dismiss us with your blessing |
| | **36 v4** | On Jordan's banks the Baptist's cry |
| 10:2-10 | **251** | O day of rest and gladness |
| 16:16ff | **217** | We place upon your table, Lord |

## DEUTERONOMY

| | | |
|---|---|---|
| 4:29 | **101** | O Christ, our king, creator, Lord |
| 5:15 | **501** | He leadeth me: oh, blessed thought! |
| 6:7 | **440** | Christians, while on earth abiding |
| 6:8 | **188** | I bind unto myself today |
| 9:26 | **333** | Lord, take my hand and lead me |
| 30:15-20 | **480** | Oh, that the Lord would guide my ways |
| 32:1-4, 7, 36a, 43 | **P. 150** | Give ear to what I say, you heavens (Ministers Edition; Attende, Caelum) |
| 32:2 | **232** | Your Word, O Lord, is gentle dew |
| 32:4 | **446** | Whatever God ordains is right |
| 33:26 | **483** | God moves in a mysterious way |

## JOSHUA

| | | |
|---|---|---|
| 1:9 | **415** | God of grace and God of glory |
| 3:13-14 | **501** | He leadeth me: oh blessed thought |
| 3:14 | **343** | Guide me ever, great Redeemer |
| 24:15b | **512** | Oh, blest the house, whate'er befall |

## 1 SAMUEL

| | | |
|---|---|---|
| 7:12 | **447** | All depends on our possessing |
| | **499** | Come, thou Fount of every blessing |

## 2 SAMUEL

| | | |
|---|---|---|
| 7:12 | **87** | Hail to the Lord's anointed |
| 22:1ff | **308** | God the Father, be our stay |

## 1 KINGS

| | | |
|---|---|---|
| 3:5-12 | **415** | God of grace and God of glory |
| 4:12 | **165 v3** | Holy, holy, holy, Lord God Almighty |
| 8:27-30 | **365 v2** | Built on a rock the Church shall stand |
| 9:3 | **367** | Christ is made the sure foundation |
| 19:9-12 | **506** | Dear Lord and Father of mankind |

## 1 CHRONICLES

| | | |
|---|---|---|
| 29:10-13 | **532** | How great thou art |
| 29:14 | **410** | We give thee but thine own |

## 2 CHRONICLES

| | | |
|---|---|---|
| 20:12 | **303** | When in the hour of deepest need |
| 29:25-30 | **251** | O day of rest and gladness |
| 31:5-6 | **404** | As saints of old their first fruits brought |

## EZRA

| | | |
|---|---|---|
| 9:6 | **310** | To you, omniscient Lord of all |

## JOB

| | | |
|---|---|---|
| 1:21 | **474** | Children of the heav'nly Father |
| 7:1-7 | **341** | Jesus, still lead on |
| 19:25-26 | **352** | I know that my Redeemer lives |
| 19:25-27 | **340** | Jesus Christ, my sure defense |
| 19:25-29 | **147** | Hallelujah, Jesus lives! |
| Ch. 38 & 39 | **483** | God moves in a mysterious way |
| 38:7 | **41** | O little town of Bethlehem |
| 38:8-11 | **467** | Eternal Father, strong to save |
| 38:31, 33 | **391** | And have the bright immensities |

## PSALMS

| | | |
|---|---|---|
| 1:3 | **232** | Your Word, O Lord, is gentle dew |
| 8:3-4 | **391** | And have the bright immensities |
| | **561** | For the beauty of the earth |
| Ch. 13 | **369** | The Church's one foundation |
| 16:1 | **239** | God's Word is our great heritage |
| 16:2 | **542** | Sing praise to God, the highest good |

## PSALMS (continued)

| | | |
|---|---|---|
| 16:5-6, 11-12 | **264** | When all your mercies, O my God |
| 16:8 | **505** | Forth in thy name, O Lord, I go |
| 16:11 | **185** | Great God, a blessing from your throne |
| 17:8 | **P. 157** | Keep me in the apple of your eye (in Prayer at the Close of Day) |
| 17:15 | **P. 157** | Keep me in the apple of your eye (in Prayer at the Close of Day) |
| Ch. 18 | **502** | Thee will I love, my strength, my tow'r |
| 18:1 | **345** | How sweet the name of Jesus sounds |
| 18:6-7, 16-17 | **Cant. 9** | I called to my God for help |
| 18:18 | **308** | God the Father, be our stay |
| 18:31-32 | **325** | Lord, thee I love with all my heart |
| 19:1-6 | **247** | Holy Majesty, before you |
| | **391** | And have the bright immensities |
| | **532** | How great thou art |
| | **561** | For the beauty of the earth |
| 19:7 | **232** | Your Word, O Lord, is gentle dew |
| 20:5 | **553** | Rejoice, O pilgrim throng! |
| Ch. 23 | **371** | With God as our friend, with his Spirit and Word |
| | **450** | Who trusts in God, a strong abode |
| | **451** | The Lord's my shepherd; I'll not want |
| | **456** | The King of love my shepherd is |
| | **481** | Savior, like a shepherd lead us |
| 23:2 | **501** | He leadeth me: oh, blessed thought! |
| 23:4 | **336** | Jesus, thy boundless love to me |
| Ch. 24 | **32** | Fling wide the door, unbar the gate |
| | **108** | All glory, laud, and honor |
| 24:7 | **536** | O God of God, O Light of Light |
| 24:7-9 | **26** | Prepare the royal highway |
| 25:7 | **414** | O God of love, O King of peace |
| 25:14 | **371** | With God as our friend, with his Spirit and Word |
| 26:12 | **241** | We praise you, O God, our redeemer, creator |
| Ch. 27 | **454** | If God himself be for me |
| 27:1 | **526** | Immortal, invisible, God only wise |
| 27:14 | **415** | God of grace and God of glory |
| 28:2 | **168** | Kyrie, God Father in heav'n above |
| 30:4-5 | **319** | Oh, sing, my soul, your maker's praise |
| 31:3 | **341** | Jesus, still lead on |
| 31:5 | **P. 156** | Into your hands, O Lord (in Prayer at the Close of Day) |
| 32:7 | **484** | God, my Lord, my strength, my place of hiding |

## PSALMS (continued)

| | | |
|---|---|---|
| 33:1, 5 | **264** | When all your mercies, O my God |
| 33:20 | **320** | O God, our help in ages past |
| 34:8 | **226** | Draw near and take the body of the Lord |
| | **516** | Arise, my soul, arise! |
| 39:12 | **211** | Here, O my Lord, I see thee face to face |
| Ch. 42 | **452** | As pants the hart for cooling streams |
| Ch. 45 | **76** | O Morning Star, how fair and bright |
| 45:2 | **518** | Beautiful Savior |
| 45:3 | **522** | Come, thou almighty King |
| Ch. 46 | **436** | All who love and serve your city |
| 46:1 | **228, 229** | A mighty fortress is our God |
| | **485** | Lord, as a pilgrim through life I go |
| 46:5 | **430** | Where restless crowds are thronging |
| 46:9 | **414** | O God of love, O King of peace |
| Ch. 48 | **358** | Glories of your name are spoken |
| | **416** | O God of ev'ry nation |
| 48:1 | **524** | My God, how wonderful thou art |
| | **532** | How Great Thou Art |
| 50:9 | **512** | Oh, blest the house, whate'er befall |
| 51:3 | **310** | To you, omniscient Lord of all |
| 51:4 | **511** | Renew me, O eternal Light |
| 51:10-12 | **P. 75, 96, 118** | Create in me a clean heart, O God |
| 51:11 | **310** | To you, omniscient Lord of all |
| 51:17 | **438** | Lord, teach us how to pray aright |
| | **469** | Lord of all hopefulness, Lord of all joy |
| 51:18 | **490** | Let me be yours forever |
| 55:22 | **453** | If you but trust in God to guide you |
| 57:1 | **278** | All praise to thee, my God, this night |
| 61:2 | **327** | Rock of Ages, cleft for me |
| 61:3 | **320** | O God, our help in ages past |
| 65:5-8 | **467** | Eternal Father, strong to save |
| 65:9-13 | **412** | Sing to the Lord of harvest |
| Ch. 67 | **335** | May God bestow on us his grace |
| 70:4 | **524** | My God, how wonderful thou art |
| | **532** | How Great Thou Art |
| 71:22f | **553** | Rejoice, O pilgrim throng! |
| Ch. 72 | **87** | Hail to the Lord's anointed |
| | **530** | Jesus shall reign where'er the sun |
| 72:6 | **409** | Praise and thanksgiving |
| 72:8, 17 | **530** | Jesus shall reign where'er the sun |
| Ch. 73 | **325** | Lord, thee I love with all my heart |
| 73:3 | **440** | Christians, while on earth abiding |
| 73:23 | **468** | From God can nothing move me |
| 73:25ff | **450** | Who trusts in God, a strong abode |

## PSALMS (continued)

| | | |
|---|---|---|
| 79:9 | **366** | Lord of our life and God of our salvation |
| 80:1 | **361** | Do not despair, O little flock |
| | **402** | Look from your sphere of endless day |
| | **450** | Who trusts in God, a strong abode |
| | **481** | Savior, like a shepherd lead us |
| | **485** | Lord as a pilgrim through life I go |
| 81:3 | **556** | Herald, sound the note of judgement |
| 82:43 | **318** | The Lord will come and not be slow |
| Ch. 85 | **519** | My soul, now praise your maker! |
| 85:8-13 | **318** | The Lord will come and not be slow |
| 86:13 | **290** | There's a wideness in God's mercy |
| 87:3 | **358** | Glories of your name are spoken |
| 89:1 | **Cant. 16** | I will sing the story of your love, O Lord |
| 89:8 | **569** | God bless our native land |
| 90:1-5 | **320** | O God, our help in ages past |
| 91:4 | **543** | Praise to the Lord, the Almighty, the King of creation! |
| 90:12-17 | **444** | With the Lord begin your task |
| 92:5 | **532** | How Great Thou Art |
| Ch. 93 | **522** | Come, thou almighty King |
| | **554** | This is my Father's world |
| 93:1 | **544** | The God of Abraham praise |
| 93:1-4 | **252** | You servants of God, your master proclaim |
| Ch. 95 | **254** | Come, let us join our cheerful songs |
| | **522** | Come, thou almighty King |
| | **Cant. 4** | Come, let us sing to the Lord |
| Ch. 96 | **558** | Earth and all stars! |
| 96:4 | **532** | How great thou art! |
| 96:10 | **124, 125** | The royal banners forward go |
| 97:6 | **527** | All creatures of our God and King |
| Ch. 98 | **39** | Joy to the world, the Lord is come! |
| 98:1 | **554** | This is my Father's world |
| | **558** | Earth and all stars! |
| 98:1, 4-9 | **527** | All creatures of our God and King |
| 98:7-9 | **39** | Joy to the world, the Lord is come! |
| 99:7 | **P. 144** | In the Service of Light (Evening Prayer) |
| Ch. 100 | **245** | All people that on earth do dwell |
| | **256** | Oh, sing jubilee to the Lord, ev'ry land |
| | **531** | Before Jehovah's awesome throne |
| | **564, 565** | Praise God, from whom all blessings flow |

PSALMS (continued)

| | | |
|---|---|---|
| 100:1 | **237** | O God of light, your Word a lamp unfailing |
| 100:4 | **250** | Open now thy gates of beauty |
| 100:5 | **Cant. 16** | I will sing the story of your love, O Lord |
| 102:25-28 | **320** | O God, our help in ages past |
| Ch. 103 | **519** | My soul, now praise your maker! |
| | **549** | Praise, my soul, the King of heaven |
| 103:1-11 | **543** | Praise to the Lord, the Almighty, the King of creation |
| Ch. 104 | **Cant. 18** | All you works of the Lord |
| | **527** | All creatures of our God and King |
| | **541** | Praise the Lord of heaven! |
| | **548** | Oh, worship the King, all-glorious above |
| | **561** | For the beauty of the earth |
| 104:1 | **524** | My God, how wonderful thou art |
| | **532** | How Great Thou Art |
| 104:33 | **538** | Oh, praise the Lord, my soul! |
| 105:2 | **385** | What wondrous love is this, O my soul, O my soul! |
| 106:1 | **470** | Praise and thanks and adoration |
| Ch. 108 | **538** | Oh, praise the Lord, my soul! |
| 108:1-2 | **269** | Awake, my soul, and with the sun |
| 113:3 | **275** | O Trinity, O blessed Light |
| | **274** | The day you gave us, Lord, has ended |
| 116:12-14, 18-19 | **P. 67, 87, 108** | Canticle, What shall I render to the Lord |
| 116:12, 17 | **561** | For the beauty of the earth |
| Ch. 117 | **550** | From all that dwell below the skies |
| 118:15 | **141 v2** | The day of resurrection! |
| 118:22 | **367** | Christ is made the sure foundation |
| 118:24 | **251** | O day of rest and gladness |
| 118:26 | **108** | All glory, laud, and honor |
| Ch. 119 | **P. 144** | In the Service of Light (Evening Prayer) |
| | **233** | Thy strong word did cleave the darkness |
| 119:5, 33, 113, 176 | **480** | Oh, that the Lord would guide my ways |
| 119:105 | **231** | O Word of God incarnate |
| | **237** | O God of light, your Word, a lamp unfailing |
| 119:111 | **239** | God's Word is our great heritage |
| 119:133 | **309** | Lord Jesus, think on me |
| Ch. 121 | **445** | Unto the hills around do I lift up |
| 121:4 | **542** | Sing praise to God, the highest good |
| 122:6-9 | **471** | Grant peace, we pray, in mercy, Lord |

## PSALMS (continued)

| | | |
|---|---|---|
| 126:3 | **560** | Oh, that I had a thousand voices |
| 126:6 | **487** | Let us ever walk with Jesus |
| Ch. 130 | **295** | Out of the depths I cry to you |
| 135:1 | **252** | You servants of God, your master proclaim |
| Ch. 136 | **520** | Give to our God immortal praise! |
| | **521** | Let us with a gladsome mind |
| 136:12 | **501** | He leadeth me: oh, blessed thought! |
| | **333** | Lord, take my hand and lead me |
| Ch. 137 | **368** | I love your kingdom, Lord |
| 139:10 | **333** | Lord, take my hand and lead me |
| | **501** | He leadeth me: oh, blessed thought! |
| 139:13-16 | **505** | Forth in thy name, O Lord, I go |
| 139:23-24 | **311** | Wondrous are your ways, O God! |
| Ch. 141 | **P. 145** | O Lord, I call to you |
| | **Cant. 5** | (Domine Clamavi) |
| 141:2 | **186** | How blessed is this place, O Lord |
| Ch. 145 | **419** | Lord of all nations, grant me grace |
| 145:1 | **401** | Before you, Lord, we bow |
| | **527** | All creatures of our God and King |
| 145:10 | **527** | All creatures of our God and King |
| Ch. 146 | **539** | Praise the Almighty, my soul, adore him! |
| Ch. 148 | **242** | Let the whole creation cry |
| | **527** | All creatures of our God and King |
| | **540** | Praise the Lord! O heav'ns adore him |
| | **541** | Praise the Lord of heaven! |
| 148:1-2 | **175** | Ye watchers and ye holy ones |
| 148:3 | **532** | How Great Thou Art |
| 149:1 | **558** | Earth and all stars! |
| Ch. 150 | **543** | Praise to the Lord, the Almighty |
| | **555** | When in our music God is glorified |
| | **560** | Oh, that I had a thousand voices |
| 150:1 | **564, 565** | Praise God from whom all blessings flow |
| 150:2 | **515** | How marvelous God's greatness |
| 150:3 | **251** | O day of rest and gladness |
| 150:6 | **557** | Let all things now living |
| | **560** | Oh, that I had a thousand voices |

## PROVERBS

| | | |
|---|---|---|
| 10:22 | **447** | All depends on our possessing |
| 18:24 | **298** | One there is, above all others |
| | **439** | What a friend we have in Jesus |

## ECCLESIASTES

| | | |
|---|---|---|
| 9:10 | **444** | With the Lord begin your task |

## ISAIAH

| | | |
|---|---|---|
| 2:2-5 | **Cant. 7** | Climb to the top of the highest mountain |
| 3:8 | **31** | Wake, awake, for night is flying |
| 5:1-2, 7 | **P. 149** | I will sing for my beloved (Vinea Facta Est) (Ministers Edition) |
| | **227** | How blest are they who hear God's word |
| 6:1-3 | **227** | How blest are they who hear God's word |
| 6:1ff | **528** | Isaiah in a vision did of old |
| 6:2 | **198** | Let all mortal flesh keep silence |
| 6:2-3 | **165** | Holy, holy, holy, Lord God Almighty! |
| | **249** | God himself is present |
| | **535** | Holy God, we praise your name |
| 6:3 | **P. 69, 89, 100** | Canticle: Holy, holy, holy, Lord (Sanctus) |
| | **242** | Let the whole creation cry |
| | **251** | O day of rest and gladness |
| | **253** | Lord Jesus Christ, be present now |
| | **547** | Thee we adore, eternal Lord! |
| 6:8 | **283** | O God, send heralds who will never falter |
| | **381** | Hark, the voice of Jesus calling |
| 7:14 | **34** | Oh, come, oh, come, Emmanuel |
| | **41** | O little town of Bethlehem |
| 9:1-2 | **Cant. 8** | The people who walked in darkness |
| 9:3 | **407** | Come, you thankful people, come |
| 9:4-5 | **54** | It came upon the midnight clear |
| 9:6 | **30** | Come, thou long-expected Jesus |
| | **60** | Hark! The herald angels sing |
| | **364** | Son of God, eternal Savior |
| 11:1 | **34** | Oh, come, oh, come, Emmanual |
| | **57** | Let our gladness have no end, Hallelujah! |
| | **58** | Lo, how a rose is growing |
| 11:2 | **164** | Creator Spirit, by whose aid |
| | **284** | Creator Spirit, heav'nly dove |
| | **459** | O Holy Spirit, enter in |
| | **472, 473** | Come, Holy Ghost, our souls inspire |
| 11:6 | **40** | What child is this, who, laid to rest |

## ISAIAH (continued)

| | | |
|---|---|---|
| 21:11 | **382** | Awake, O Spirit of the watchmen |
| 25:6 | **516** | Arise, my soul, arise! |
| 28:16 | **367** | Christ is made the sure foundation |
| | **507** | How firm a foundation, O saints of the Lord |
| 30:15 | **506** | Dear Lord and Father of mankind |
| 30:18b | **437** | Not alone for mighty empire |
| 32:2 | **107** | Beneath the cross of Jesus |
| 33:20-21 | **358** | Glories of your name are spoken |
| Ch. 35 | **384** | Your Kingdom come, O Father |
| | **401** | Before you, Lord, we bow |
| | **402** | Look from your sphere of endless day |
| 35:1-10 | **87** | Hail to the Lord's anointed |
| 39:8 | **462** | God the omnipotent! King who ordainest |
| 39:12 | **343** | Guide me ever, great Redeemer |
| | **485** | Lord, as a pilgrim through life I go |
| | **498** | All who would valiant be |
| 40:1-8 | **29** | Comfort, comfort now my people |
| 40:3 | **35** | Hark, the glad sound! The Savior comes |
| | **36** | On Jordan's banks the Baptist's cry |
| | **556** | Herald, sound the note of judgement |
| 40:3-4 | **26** | Prepare the royal highway |
| 40:3-5 | **25** | Rejoice, rejoice, believers |
| 40:3, 7 | **36** | On Jordan's banks the Baptist's cry |
| 40:6-8 | **519** | My soul, now praise your maker |
| 40:9 | **Cant. 7** | Climb to the top of the highest mountain |
| | **556** | Herald, sound the note of judgement |
| 40:11 | **193** | Cradling children in his arm |
| | **474** | Children of the heav'nly Father |
| | **507** | How firm a foundation, O saints of the Lord |
| 40:20b-21 | **394** | Lost in the night do the people yet languish |
| 40:21 | **543** | Praise to the Lord, the Almighty, the King of creation! |
| 40:22 | **463** | God, who stretched the spangled heavens |
| 40:26 | **567** | God of our fathers, whose almighty hand |
| 40:28 | **543 v2** | Praise to the Lord, the Almighty, the King of creation! |
| 40:31 | **543 v2** | Praise to the Lord, the Almighty, the King of creation! |
| 41:8 | **544 v3** | The God of Abr'ham praise |

| | | |
|---|---|---|
| 41:10 | 507 | How firm a foundation, O saints of the Lord |
| 42:5-12 | 542 | Sing praise to God, the highest good |
| 42:10 | Cant. 10 | Sing praise to the Lord, all the earth |
| 43:1-7 | 507 | How firm a foundation, O saints of the Lord |
| 48:18 | 346 | When peace, like a river |
| 49:1 | Cant. 14 | Listen! You nations of the world |
| 49:11 | 70 | Go tell it on the mountain |
| 49:13 | 540 | Praise the Lord! O heav'ns, adore him |
| 49:16 | 368 | I love your kingdom, Lord |
| 52:1-8 | 31 | Wake, awake, for night is flying |
| 52:7 | 396 | O God, O Lord of heav'n and earth |
| 52:7-10 | 70 | Go tell it on the mountain |
| 52:8 | 382 | Awake, O Spirit of the watchmen |
| Ch. 53 | 38 | Alas, and did my Savior bleed |
| | 97 | Christ, the life of all the living |
| | 98 | Alas, and did my Savior bleed |
| | 100 | Deep were his wounds, and red |
| | 123 | Ah, holy Jesus, how hast thou offended |
| 53:4-7 | 105 | A lamb goes uncomplaining forth |
| | 116, 117 | O sacred head, now wounded |
| 53:6 | 305 | I lay my sins on Jesus |
| 55:6-11 | Cant. 15 | Seek the Lord while he may be found (Quaerite Dominum) |
| 55:10-11 | 232 | Your Word, O Lord, is gentle dew |
| 55:13 | 39 | Joy to the world, the Lord is come! |
| 57:15 | 365 | Built on a rock the church shall stand |
| | 526 | Immortal, invisible, God only wise |
| 58:5-9 | 423 | Lord, whose love in humble service |
| 59:20 | 34 | Oh, come, oh, come, Emmanuel |
| 60:1ff | 393 | Rise, shine, you people! Christ the Lord has entered |
| 60:1-2 | Cant. 8 | The people who walked in darkness |
| 60:5 | Cant. 14 | Listen! You nations of the world |
| 60:19 | 82 | As with gladness men of old |
| 61:1-2 | 35 | Hark, the glad sound! The Savior comes |
| | 312 | Once he came in blessing |
| 61:10 | 224 | Soul, adorn yourself with gladness |
| | 302 | Jesus, your blood and righteousness |
| 63:3 | 332 | Battle Hymn of the Republic |
| 63:9 | 96 | Your heart, O God, is grieved |
| 64:4 | 31 | Wake, awake, for night is flying |
| 66:10-14 | 519 | My soul, now praise your maker! |

## JEREMIAH

| | | |
|---|---|---|
| 1:4-10 | 510 | O God of youth, whose Spirit in our hearts is stirring |
| 17:5-8 | 378 | Amid the world's bleak wilderness |
| 17:7 | 460 | I am trusting you, Lord Jesus |
| 22:29 | 401 v4 | Before you, Lord, we bow |
| 31:7-14 | Cant. 14 | Listen! You nations of the world |
| 33:11 | Cant. 16 | I will sing the story of your love, O Lord |
| 33:14-16 | 34 | Oh, come, oh, come, Emmanuel |

## LAMENTATIONS

| | | |
|---|---|---|
| 1:12 | 93 | Jesus, refuge of the weary |
| 3:19 | 109 | Go to dark Gethsemane |
| 3:22-23 | Cant. 12 | God, who has called you to glory |
| | 453 | If you but trust in God to guide you |

## EZEKIEL

| | | |
|---|---|---|
| 1:26 | 121 | Ride on, ride on in majesty |
| 3:17 | 31 | Wake, awake, for night is flying |
| 33:6 | 382 | Awake, O Spirit of the watchmen |
| Ch. 34 | 371 | With God as our friend, with his Spirit and Word |
| | 402 | Look from your sphere of endless day |
| | 451 | The Lord's my shepherd; I'll not want |
| | 456 | The King of love my shepherd is |
| | 481 | Savior, like a shepherd lead us |
| 36:26 | 484 | God, my Lord, my strength, my place of hiding |

## DANIEL

| | | |
|---|---|---|
| 2:35 | 274 | The day you gave us, Lord, has ended |
| 4:13 | 175 | Ye watchers and ye holy ones |
| 7:9-10 | 314 | Who is this host arrayed in white |
| 7:13 | 526 | Immortal, invisible, God only wise |
| | 544 | The God of Abr'ham praise |
| 7:13-14 | 522 | Come, thou almighty King |

## JOEL

| | | |
|---|---|---|
| 2:13 | P. 93, 83, 104 | Return to the Lord your God (in the Orders for Holy Communion) |

**MICAH**

| 5:2 | 41 | O little town of Bethlehem |

**HABAKKUK**

| 2:20 | 198 | Let all mortal flesh keep silence |
| | 249 | God himself is present |

**ZEPHANIAH**

| 3:14-20 | 341 | Jesus, still lead on |

**ZECHARIAH**

| 4:6 | 437 v2 | Not alone for mighty empire |
| 4:8 | 228,229 | A mighty fortress is our God |
| 9:9 | 22 | The advent of our God |
| | 121 | Ride on, ride on in majesty! |
| 13:1 | 301 | Come to Calv'ry's holy mountain |

**MALACHI**

| 4:1-2a | 418 | Judge eternal, throned in splendor |
| 4:2 | 38 | O Savior, rend the heavens wide |
| | 60 | Hark! The herald angels sing |
| | 77 | O one with God the Father |
| | 265 | Christ, whose glory fills the skies |
| | 418 | Judge eternal, throned in splendor |

**SIRACH (Ecclus.)**

| 50:22-24 | 533 | Now thank we all our God |

**SONG OF THE THREE YOUNG MEN**

| | Cant. 18 | All you works of the Lord |
| | 527 | All creatures of our God and King |

**MATTHEW**

| 1:21, 25 | | See Topical Index: NAME OF JESUS, THE |
| 1:23 | 83 | From God the Father, virgin-born |

## MATTHEW (continued)

| | | |
|---|---|---|
| Ch. 2 | 40 | What child is this, who laid to rest |
| | 69 | I am so glad each Christmas Eve |
| | 71 | Angels we have heard on high |
| 2:1-2 | 90 | Songs of thankfulness and praise |
| 2:1-3 | 50 | Angels, from the realms of glory |
| 2:1-11 | 56 | The first Noel the angel did say |
| | 68 | He whom shepherds once came praising |
| | 69 | I am so glad each Christmas Eve |
| | 75 | Bright and glorious is the sky |
| | 81 | O chief of cities, Bethlehem |
| | 82 | As with gladness men of old |
| | 84 | Brightest and best of the stars of the morning |
| 2:1-12 | 85 | When Christ's appearing was made known |
| 2:11 | 71 | Angels we have heard on high |
| 2:16-18 | 177 v9 | By all your saints in warfare |
| 3:1-6 | 36 | On Jordan's banks the Baptist's cry |
| | 178 v15 | By all your saints in warfare |
| 3:9 | 74 | A stable lamp is lighted |
| 3:13-17 | 79 | To Jordan came the Christ, our Lord |
| | 85 | When Christ's appearing was made known |
| | 90 | Songs of thankfulness and praise |
| | 486 | Spirit of God, descend upon my heart |
| 3:16-17 | 373 | Eternal Ruler of the ceaseless round |
| 4:1-11 | 90 | Songs of thankfulness and praise |
| | 91 | Savior, when indust to you |
| | 99 | O Lord, throughout these forty days |
| | 450 | Who trusts in God, a strong abode |
| 4:18-19 | 494 | Jesus call us; o'er the tumult |
| 4:18-22 | 449 | They cast their nets in Galilee |
| | 455 | "Come, follow me," the Savior spake |
| 4:23-25 | 417 | In a lowly manger born |
| 5:1-12 | Cant. 17 | How blest are they who know their need |
| 5:42 | 424 | Lord of glory, you have bought us |
| 6:9-15 | P. 112 | Our Father in Heaven (Holy Communion III only) |
| | 442 | O thou, who hast of thy pure grace |
| 6:10 | 353 | May we your precepts, Lord, fulfill |
| | 376 | Your kingdom come! O Father, hear our prayer |
| | 384 | Your kingdom come, O Father |
| | 405 | Lord of light, your name outshining |
| | 413 | Father eternal, ruler of creation |

## MATTHEW (continued)

| | | |
|---|---|---|
| 6:12 | 307 | Forgive our sins as we forgive |
| 6:24-34 | 362 | We plow the fields and scatter |
| | 447 | All depends on our possessing |
| | 474 | Children of the Heav'nly Father |
| 7:11 | 163 | Come, Holy Ghost, God and Lord |
| | 478 | Come, oh, come, O Quick'ning Spirit |
| 7:21-29 | 299 | Dear Christians, one and all, rejoice |
| | 454 | If God himself be for me |
| 7:24-27 | 293, 294 | My hope is built on nothing less |
| | 507 | How firm a foundation |
| 8:11 | 313 | A multitude comes from the east and the west |
| | 359 | In Christ there is no east or west |
| 8:16-17 | 431 | Your hand, O Lord, in days of old |
| 8:17 | 100 | Deep were his wounds, and red |
| 8:23-25 | 360 | O Christ, the healer, we have come |
| 8:23-27 | 334 | Jesus, Savior, pilot me |
| | 467 | Eternal Father, strong to save |
| 9:9 | 178 v18 | By all your saints in warfare |
| 9:20-22 | 427 | O Jesus Christ, may grateful hymns be rising |
| 9:25 | 333 | Lord, take my hand and lead me |
| 9:37 | 381 | Hark, the voice of Jesus calling |
| 10:22 | 490 | Let me be yours forever |
| 10:38 | 398 | "Take up your cross," the Savior said |
| | 406 | Take my life, that I may be |
| | 455 | "Come, follow me," the Savior spake |
| | 504 | O God, my faithful God |
| 10:42 | 429 v4 | Where cross the crowded ways of life |
| 11:2-6 | 538 | Oh, praise the Lord, my soul! |
| 11:5 | 94 | My song is love unknown |
| 11:19 | 298 | One there is, above all others |
| 11:21 | 91 | Savior, when in dust to you |
| 11:28 | 280 | Now the day is over |
| | 301 | Come to Calv'ry's holy mountain |
| | 497 v1 | I heard the voice of Jesus say |
| | 530 | Jesus shall reign where'er the sun |
| 11:28-30 | 305 | I lay my sins on Jesus |
| | 439 | What a friend we have in Jesus |
| 11:29 | 455 | "Come, follow me," the Savior spake |
| 11:29-30 | 505 | Forth in thy name, O Lord, I go |
| 12:29 | 228, 229 | A mighty fortress is our God |
| 12:39 | 392 | O Lord, send forth your Spirit |
| 13:3, 18-23 | 261 | On what has now been sown |

## MATTHEW (continued)

| | | |
|---|---|---|
| 13:3-9, 18-23 | 234 | Almighty God, your Word is cast |
| | 250 | Open now thy gates of beauty |
| 13:8, 23 | 236 | When seed falls on good soil |
| 13:24-30, 37-40 | 407 | Come, you thankful people, come |
| 13:45, 46 | 457, 458 | Jesus, priceless treasure |
| 14:13-33 | 235 | Break now the bread of life |
| | 333 | Lord, take my hand and lead me |
| | 334 | Jesus, Savior, pilot me |
| | 457, 458 | Jesus, priceless treasure |
| 14:22-33 | 334 | Jesus, Savior, pilot me |
| | 467 | Eternal Father, strong to save |
| 14:36 | 427 v3 | O Jesus Christ, may grateful hymns be rising |
| 15:22 | 310 | To you, omniscient Lord of all |
| 15:29-31 | 426 | O Son of God, in Galilee |
| 15:31 | 446 | Whatever God ordains is right |
| 16:1 | 392 | O Lord, send forth your spirit |
| 16:13-20 | 177 (v10) | By all your saints in warfare |
| 16:13-23 | 365 | Built on a rock the Church shall stand |
| 16:18 | 509 | Onward, Christian soldiers |
| 16:24 | 398 | "Take up your cross," the Savior said |
| | 455 | "Come, follow me," the Savior spake |
| | 470 | Praise and thanks and adoration |
| 17:1-8 | 80 | Oh, wondrous type! Oh, vision fair |
| | 89 | How good, Lord, to be here! |
| Ch. 18 | 365 v3 | Built on a rock the Church shall stand |
| 18:12 | 291 v3 | Jesus sinners will receive |
| 18:14 | 397 | O Zion, haste, your mission high fulfilling |
| 18:20 | 391 | And have the bright immensities |
| 18:21-35 | 126 | Where charity and love prevail |
| 19:6 | 287 | O perfect Love, all human thought transcending |
| 19:13-15 | 187 | Dearest Jesus, we are here |
| | 193 | Cradling children in his arm |
| 19:20 | 455 | "Come, follow me," the Savior spake |
| 20:1-16 | 381 | Hark, the voice of Jesus calling |
| 20:17-19 | 115 | Jesus, I will ponder now |
| | 132 | Come, you faithful, raise the strain |
| 20:22 | 183 | The Son of God goes forth to war |
| 20:28 | 24 | Come, O precious Ransom, come |

## MATTHEW (continued)

| | | |
|---|---|---|
| | 283 | O God, send heralds who will never falter |
| 21:1-9 | 121 | Ride on, ride on in majesty! |
| | 23 | O Lord, how shall I meet you |
| 21:5 | 24 | Come, O precious Ransom, come |
| 21:6-9, 15 | 108 | All glory, laud, and honor |
| 21:8-9 | 23 | O Lord, how shall I meet you |
| | 26 | Prepare the royal highway |
| | 94 | My song is love unknown |
| | 258 | Hosanna to the living Lord! |
| 21:22 | 439 | What a friend we have in Jesus |
| 21:42 | 367 | Christ is made the sure foundation |
| | 369 | The Church's one foundation |
| 22:9 | 429 | Where cross the crowded ways of life |
| 22:34-40 | 325 | Lord, thee I love with all my heart |
| 22:37 | 486 | Spirit of God, descend upon my heart |
| | 494 | Jesus call us; o'er the tumult |
| 24:29-31 | 321 | The day is surely drawing near |
| 24:31 | 293, 294 v4 | My hope is built on nothing less |
| 24:35 | 356 | O Jesus, joy of loving hearts |
| Ch. 25 | 410 v2 | We give thee but thine own |
| 25:1-13 | 25 | Rejoice, rejoice, believers |
| | 31 | Wake, awake, for night is flying |
| | 224 | Soul, adorn yourself with gladness |
| 25:31 | 410 v6 | We give thee but thine own |
| | 424 | Lord of glory, you have bought us |
| 25:40 | 425 | O God of mercy, God of light |
| 26:26-28 | 120 | Of the glorious body telling |
| | 197 | O living Bread from heaven |
| | 198 | Let all mortal flesh keep silence |
| | 200 | For the bread which you have broken |
| | 208 | Lord Jesus Christ, you have prepared |
| | 209 | Come, risen Lord, and deign to be our guest |
| | 210 | At the Lamb's high feast we sing |
| | 496 | Around you, O Lord Jesus |
| 26:39 | 183 | The Son of God goes forth to war |
| 26:36-46 | 106 | In the hour of trial |
| 26:41 | 286 v4 | Bow down your ear, almighty Lord |
| | 443 | Rise, my soul to watch and pray |
| Ch. 27 | 123 | Ah, holy Jesus, how hast thou offended |
| 27:21-22 | 94 | My song is love unknown |
| 27:27-31 | 116, 117 | O sacred head, now wounded |
| | 156 v3 | Look, oh look, the sight is glorious |

## MATTHEW (continued)

| | | |
|---|---|---|
| 27:33ff | 100 | Deep were his wounds, and |
| | 114 | There is a green hill far away |
| 27:39-40 | 93 | Jesus, refuge of the weary |
| 27:33-35 | 301 | Come to Calv'ry's holy mountain |
| 27:33-46 | 97 | Christ, the life of all the living |
| 27:37 | 102 | On my heart imprint your image |
| 27:45 | 130 | Christ the Lord is ris'n today! |
| 27:45-46 | 74 | A stable lamp is lighted |
| 27:45, 51 | 101 | O Christ, our king, creator, Lord |
| 27:45-56 | 98 | Alas! And did my Savior bleed |
| 27:46 | 112, 113, part IV | Jesus, in thy dying woes |
| 27:50 | 97 | Christ, the life of all the living |
| | 112, 113, part IV | Jesus, in thy dying woes |
| 27:50, 60 | 91 | Savior when in dust to you |
| 27:63 | 135 | The strife is o'er, the battle done |
| 27:66 | 123 | Come, you faithful, raise the strain |
| 28:1 | 139 | O sons and daughters of the King |
| | 251 v2 | O day of rest and gladness |
| 28:1-7 | 137 | Christians, to the paschal victim |
| | 154 | That Easter day with joy was bright |
| 28:2 | 145 | Thine is the glory |
| 28:6 | 92 | Were you there when they crucified my Lord? |
| | 128 | Christ the Lord is ris'n today; Alleluia! |
| | 130 | Christ the Lord is ris'n today! |
| | 151 | Jesus Christ is ris'n today |
| | 170 | Crown him with many crowns |
| 28:9 | 141 | The day of resurrection! |
| 28:18, 20 | 363 | Christ is alive! Let Christians sing |
| 28:19 | 79 v5 | To Jordan came the Christ, our Lord |
| | 192 | Baptized into your name most holy |
| 28:20 | 158 v2 | Alleluia! Sing to Jesus |

## MARK

| | | |
|---|---|---|
| 1:1-6 | 36 | On Jordan's banks the Baptist's cry |
| 1:2-6 | 178 v15 | By all your saints in warfare |
| 1:8-11 | 79 | To Jordan came the Christ, our Lord |
| | 85 | When Christ's appearing was made known |
| | 90 | Songs of thankfulness and praise |
| | 373 | Eternal Ruler of the ceaseless round |
| | 486 | Spirit of God, descend upon my heart |
| 1:12-13 | 90 | Songs of thankfulness and praise |
| | 91 | Savior, when in dust to you |

## MARK (continued)

| | | |
|---|---|---|
| | **99** | O Lord, throughout these forty days |
| 1:16-20 | **449** | They cast their nets in Galilee |
| | **494** | Jesus call us; o'er the tumult |
| 1:29-45 | **400** | God, whose almighty word |
| | **431** | Your hand, O Lord, in days of old |
| | **435** | O God, whose will is life and good |
| 2:12 | **448** | Amazing grace, how sweet the sound |
| 2:13-14 | **178 v15** | By all your saints in warfare |
| 3:27 | **228,** | |
| | **229** | A mighty fortress is our God |
| 4:3-9, 13-20 | **234** | Almighty God, your Word is cast |
| | **236** | When seed falls on good soil |
| | **261** | On what has now been sown |
| 4:35-41 | **333** | Lord, take my hand and lead me |
| | **334** | Jesus, Savior, pilot me |
| 5:15 | **506** | Dear Lord and Father of mankind |
| 6:47-51 | **334** | Jesus, Savior, pilot me |
| | **467** | Eternal Father, strong to save |
| 6:56 | **427 v3** | O Jesus Christ, may grateful hymns be rising |
| 7:4 | **381** | Hark, the voice of Jesus calling |
| 7:24-25 | **507** | How firm a foundation, O saints of the Lord |
| 7:32-37 | **380** | O Christ, our light, O Radiance true |
| | **426** | O Son of God, in Galilee |
| 7:37 | **446** | Whatever God ordains is right |
| 8:11-12 | **392** | O Lord, send forth your Spirit |
| 8:27-35 | **177 (v10)** | By all your saints in warfare |
| 8:34 | **398** | "Take up your cross," the Savior said |
| | **406** | Take my life, that I may be |
| | **455** | "Come follow me," the Savior spake |
| | **504** | O God, my faithful God |
| 9:2-6 | **80** | Oh, wondrous type! Oh, vision fair |
| | **89** | How good, Lord, to be here! |
| 10:8-9 | **287** | O perfect Love, all human thought transcending |
| 10:13-16 | **187** | Dearest Jesus, we are here |
| 10:14b-16 | **193** | Cradling children in his arm |
| 10:16 | **333** | Lord, take my hand and lead me |
| 10:21 | **455** | "Come, follow me," the Savior spake |
| 10:32-34 | **115** | Jesus, I will ponder now |
| | **132** | Come, you faithful, raise the strain |
| 10:45 | **24** | Come, O precious Ransom, come |
| | **283** | O God, send heralds who will never falter |

MARK (continued)

| | | |
|---|---|---|
| 10:46-52 | 426 | O Son of God, in Galilee |
| 11:1-10 | 23 | O Lord, how shall I meet you |
| | 121 | Ride on, ride on in majesty! |
| 11:8-10 | 23 | O Lord, how shall I meet you |
| | 26 | Prepare the royal highway |
| | 94 | My song is love unknown |
| | 108 | All glory, laud, and honor |
| | 258 | Hosanna to the living Lord! |
| 11:24 | 439 | What a friend we have in Jesus |
| 12:10 | 367 | Christ is made the sure foundation |
| | 369 | The Church's one foundation |
| 12:28-34 | 325 | Lord, thee I love with all my heart |
| 12:30 | 486 | Spirit of God, descend upon my heart |
| | 494 | Jesus calls us; o'er the tumult |
| 12:41-44 | 406 | Take my life, that I may be |
| 13:11 | 478 | Come, oh, come, O quick'ning Spirit |
| 13:13 | 230 | Lord, keep us steadfast in your Word |
| 13:24-27 | 313 | A multitude comes from the east and the west |
| | 321 | The day is surely drawing near |
| 13:27 | 293, 294, v4 | My hope is built on nothing less |
| 13:31 | 356 | O Jesus, joy of loving hearts |
| 14:22-25 | 120 | Of the glorious body telling |
| | 197 | O living Bread from heaven |
| | 198 | Let all mortal flesh keep silence |
| | 200 | For the bread which you have broken |
| | 208 | Lord Jesus Christ, you have prepared |
| | 209 | Come, risen Lord and deign to be our guest |
| | 210 | At the Lamb's high feast we sing |
| | 496 | Around you, O Lord Jesus |
| 14:26 | 555 | When in our music God is glorified |
| 14:32-42ff | 106 | In the hour of trial |
| | 109 | Go to dark Gethsemane |
| 14:38 | 286 v4 | Bow down your ear, almighty Lord |
| | 443 | Rise, my soul, to watch and pray |
| 14:40 | 446 | Whatever God ordains is right |
| Ch. 15 | 92 | Were you there when they crucified my Lord? |
| | 112, 113 | Jesus in thy dying woes |
| 15:12-14 | 94 | My song is love unknown |
| | 123 | Ah, holy Jesus, how hast thou offended |
| 15:16-20 | 116, 117 | O sacred head, now wounded |
| | 156 v3 | Look, oh look, the sight is glorious |

## MARK (continued)

| | | |
|---|---|---|
| 15:22ff | 97 | Christ, the life of all the living |
| | 114 | There is a green hill far away |
| | 100 | Deep were his wounds, and red |
| | 301 v1 | Come to Calv'ry's holy mountain |
| 15:29-30 | 93 | Jesus, refuge of the weary |
| 15:26 | 102 | On my heart imprint your image |
| 15:33 | 130 | Christ the Lord is ris'n today! |
| 15:33, 37 | 98 | Alas! And did my Savior bleed |
| 15:33, 38 | 101 | O Christ, our king, creator, Lord |
| 15:33-34 | 74 | A stable lamp is lighted |
| 15:34 | 112, part IV | Jesus, in thy dying woes |
| 15:37, 46 | 91 | Savior, when in dust to you |
| | 113 | Jesus, in thy dying woes |
| 16:1-2 | 139 | O sons and daughters of the King |
| | 251 v2 | O day of rest and gladness |
| 16:1-8 | 92 | Were you there when they crucified my Lord? |
| | 130 | Christ the Lord is ris'n today! |
| | 137 | Christians, to the paschal victim |
| | 145 | Thine is the glory |
| | 151 | Jesus Christ is ris'n today |
| | 154 | That Easter day with joy was bright |
| | 170 | Crown him with many crowns |
| 16:6 | 128 | Christ the Lord is ris'n today; Alleluia! |
| 16:16 | 194 | All who believe and are baptized |

## LUKE

| | | |
|---|---|---|
| 1:26-31 | 64 | From east to west, from shore to shore |
| 1:46-55 | P. 147 | The Gospel Canticle for Evening Prayer |
| | Cant. 6 | My soul proclaims the greatness of the Lord |
| | 180 | My soul now magnifies the Lord |
| 1:57-67 | 177 (v15) | By all your saints in warfare |
| 1:67 | P. 134 | The Gospel Canticle for Morning Prayer |
| | Cant. 2 | Blessed be the Lord |
| 1:70 | 380 | O Christ, our light, O Radiance true |
| 1:76-79 | 43 | Rejoice, rejoice this happy morn |
| 1:78 | 265 | Christ, whose glory fills the skies |
| Ch. 2 | 71 | Angels we have heard on high |
| | 259 | Lord, dismiss us with your blessing |
| 2:1-14 | 47 | Let all together praise our God |
| 2:1-20 | 40 | What child is this, who laid to rest |
| 2:5-7 | 48 | All praise to you, eternal Lord |
| 2:7 | 55 | Good Christian friends, rejoice |

## LUKE (continued)

| | | |
|---|---|---|
| | 59 | When Christmas morn is dawning |
| | 67 | Away in a manger, no crib for his bed |
| 2:7-11 | 64 | From east to west, from shore to shore |
| 2:7-14 | 50 | Angels, from the realms of glory |
| 2:7-15 | 65 | Silent night, holy night! |
| 2:7-20 | 44 | Infant holy, infant lowly |
| | 51 | From heaven above to earth I come |
| | 66 | Come rejoicing, praises voicing |
| | 68 | He whom shepherds once came praising |
| | 69 | I am so glad each Christmas Eve |
| | 70 | Go tell it on the mountain |
| | 71 | Angels we have heard on high |
| | 74 | A stable lamp is lighted |
| 2:7, 40 | 417 | In a lowly manger born |
| 2:8-9 | 56 | The first Noel the angel did say |
| 2:8-14 | 46 | Once again my heart rejoices |
| 2:9-12 | 63 | From shepherding of stars that gaze |
| 2:10-14 | 43 | Rejoice, rejoice this happy morn |
| 2:13-14 | 54 | It came upon the midnight clear |
| 2:14 | P. 58, 79, 100 | Glory to God in the highest (from the Holy Communion settings) |
| | 60 | Hark! The herald angels sing |
| | 166 | All glory be to God on high |
| | 536 | O God of God, O Light of Light |
| 2:15 | 45 | Oh, come, all ye faithful |
| 2:21 | | See Topical Index, Name of Jesus, The |
| | 43 | Rejoice, rejoice this happy morn |
| 2:22-38 | 184 | In his temple now behold him |
| 2:29-32 | P. 73, 93, 116 | Lord, now you let your servant go in peace (in the Orders for Holy Communion) |
| | P. 159 | Gospel Canticle for Compline |
| | 30 | Come, thou long-expected Jesus |
| | 259 | Lord, dismiss us with your blessing |
| | 339 | O Lord, now let your servant |
| | 349 | I leave as you have promised, Lord |
| 2:41-52 | 357 | Our Father, by whose name |
| | 512 | Oh, blest the house, whate'er befall |
| 3:1-6 | 36 | On Jordan's banks the Baptist's cry |
| 3:2b-6 | 178 v15 | By all your saints in warfare |
| 3:8 | 74 | A stable lamp is lighted |
| 3:21-22 | 79 | To Jordan came the Christ, our Lord |
| | 85 | When Christ's appearing was made known |
| | 90 | Songs of thankfulness and praise |

## LUKE (continued)

| | | |
|---|---|---|
| | 373 | Eternal Ruler of the ceaseless round |
| | 486 | Spirit of God, descend upon my heart |
| 4:1-13 | 90 | Songs of thankfulness and praise |
| | 91 | Savior, when in dust to you |
| | 99 | O Lord, throughout these forty days |
| | 450 | Who trusts in God, a strong abode |
| 4:16-30 | 402 | Look from your sphere of endless day |
| 4:40 | 431 | Your hand, O Lord, in days of old |
| 4:18-19 | 35 | Hark, the glad sound! The Savior comes |
| | 312 | Once he came in blessing |
| 5:1-11 | 434 | The Son of God, our Christ, the Word, the Way |
| | 494 | Jesus calls us; o'er the tumult |
| 5:26 | 448 | Amazing grace, how sweet the sound |
| 5:27-28 | 178 v18 | By all your saints in warfare |
| 6:17-26 | Cant. 17 | How blest are those who know their need |
| 6:27-38 | 419 | Lord of all nations, grant me grace |
| 6:35-36 | 424 v1 | Lord of Glory, you have bought us |
| 6:46-48 | 293, 294 | My hope is built on nothing less |
| | 507 | How firm a foundation, O saints of the Lord |
| 7:18-23 | 538 | Oh, praise the Lord, my soul! |
| 7:22 | 94 | My song is love unknown |
| | 426 | O Son of God, in Galilee |
| 7:34 | 298 | One there is, above all others |
| | 439 | What a friend we have in Jesus |
| 8:8, 15 | 236 | When seed falls on good soil |
| 8:4-8, 11-15 | 234 | Almighty God, your Word is cast |
| | 261 | On what has now been sown |
| 8:22-25 | 334 | Jesus, Savior, pilot me |
| 8:35 | 506 | Dear Lord and Father of mankind |
| 9:11 | 177, 178 | By all your saints in warfare |
| 9:23 | 398 | "Take up your cross," the Savior said |
| | 455 | "Come, follow me," the Savior spake |
| 9:28-36 | 80 | Oh, wondrous type! Oh, vision fair |
| | 89 | How good, Lord, to be here! |
| 10:2 | 381 | Hark, the voice of Jesus calling |
| 10:13 | 91 | Savior, when in dust to you |
| 10:27 | 486 | Spirit of God, descend upon my heart |
| | 494 | Jesus calls us; o'er the tumult |
| 10:36 | 425 | O God of mercy, God of light |
| 11:1 | 438 | Lord, teach us how to pray aright |

## LUKE (continued)

| | | |
|---|---|---|
| 11:2 | **376** | Your kingdom come! O Father hear our prayer |
| | **384** | Your kingdom come, O Father |
| 11:2-4 | **P. 112** | Our Father in heaven (Holy Communion III only) |
| | **442** | O thou, who hast of thy pure grace |
| 11:3 | **413** | Father eternal, ruler of creation |
| 11:4 | **307** | Forgive our sins as we forgive |
| 11:13 | **163** | Come, Holy Ghost, God and Lord |
| | **478** | Come, oh, come, O quick'ning Spirit |
| 11:16 | **392** | O Lord, send forth your Spirit |
| 11:21 | **228, 229** | A mighty fortress is our God |
| 11:28 | **227** | How blest are they who hear God's Word |
| | **248** | Dearest Jesus, at your word |
| 11:29 | **392** | O Lord, send forth your Spirit |
| 12:13-21 | **364** | Son of God, eternal Savior |
| | **447** | All depends on our possessing |
| 12:22-34 | **453** | If you but trust in God to guide you |
| 12:24 | **362** | We plow the fields and scatter |
| 12:32 | **361** | Do not despair, O little flock |
| | **476** | Have no fear, little flock |
| 13:29 | **313** | A multitude comes from the east and the west |
| | **359** | In Christ there is no east or west |
| 13:31-35 | **427** | O Jesus Christ, may grateful hymns be rising |
| 14:15-24 | **313** | A multitude comes from the east and the west |
| 14:17 | **208** | Lord Jesus Christ, you have prepared |
| | **213** | I come, O Savior, to your table |
| | **214** | Come, let us eat, for now the feast is spread |
| | **496** | Around you, O Lord Jesus |
| 14:23 | **429** | Where cross the crowded ways of life |
| 14:27 | **398** | "Take up your cross," the Savior said |
| | **406** | Take my life, that I may be |
| | **455** | "Come, follow me," the Savior spake |
| | **504** | O God, my faithful God |
| 15:2-4 | **291 v3** | Jesus sinners will receive |
| 15:4-10 | **243** | Lord, with glowing heart I'd praise thee |
| | **448** | Amazing grace, how sweet the sound |
| 15:11-32 | **372** | In Adam we have all been one |
| | **506** | Dear Lord and Father of mankind |
| 15:20-24 | **304** | Today your mercy calls us |
| 17:3-4 | **307** | Forgive our sins as we forgive |

## LUKE (continued)

| | | |
|---|---|---|
| 17:13 | **111** | Lamb of God, pure and sinless |
| 18:13 | **91** | Savior, when in dust to you |
| | **296** | Just as I am, without one plea |
| | **310** | To you, omniscient Lord of all |
| 18:15-17 | **187** | Dearest Jesus, we are here |
| | **193** | Cradling children in his arm |
| 18:17 | **474** | Children of the heav'nly Father |
| 18:22 | **455** | "Come, follow me," the Savior spake |
| 18:31-34 | **115** | Jesus, I will ponder now |
| 18:31-43 | **487** | Let us ever walk with Jesus |
| 18:33 | **132** | Come, you faithful, raise the strain |
| 19:1-10 | **304** | Today your mercy calls us |
| 19:12ff | **410 v2** | We give thee but thine own |
| 19:28-40 | **74** | A stable lamp is lighted |
| | **355** | Through the night of doubt and sorrow |
| 19:37-38 | **23** | O Lord, how shall I meet you |
| | **26** | Prepare the royal highway |
| | **94** | My song is love unknown |
| | **108** | All glory, laud, and honor |
| | **258** | Hosanna to the living Lord! |
| 19:41 | **429** | Where cross the crowded ways of life |
| 19:41-44 | **427** | O Jesus Christ, may grateful hymns be rising |
| 20:17 | **367** | Christ is made the sure foundation |
| 21:10-19 | **361** | Do not despair, O little flock |
| 21:25-36 | **37** | Hark! A thrilling voice is sounding |
| 21:25-36 | **321** | The day is surely drawing near |
| 22:14-19 | **120** | Of the glorious body telling |
| 22:19 | **197** | O living Bread from heaven |
| | **198** | Let all mortal flesh keep silence |
| | **200** | For the bread which you have broken |
| | **208** | Lord Jesus Christ, you have prepared |
| | **209** | Come, risen Lord and deign to be our guest |
| | **210** | At the Lamb's high feast we sing |
| | **496** | Around you, O Lord Jesus |
| 22:31-32 | **106** | In the hour of trial |
| | **120** | Of the glorious body telling |
| 22:40ff | **106** | In the hour of trial |
| | **109** | Go to dark Gethsemane |
| 23:8 | **392** | O Lord, send forth your Spirit |
| 23:20-24 | **94** | My song is love unknown |
| | **123** | Ah, holy Jesus, how hast thou offended |
| 23:33ff | **97** | Christ, the life of all the living |
| | **100** | Deep were his wounds, and red |
| | **114** | There is a green hill far away |
| | **301** | Come to Calv'ry's holy mountain |

## LUKE (continued)

| | | |
|---|---|---|
| 23:33, 53 | **92** | Were you there when they crucified my Lord? |
| 23:34 | **112, 113** | Jesus, in thy dying woes |
| 23:38 | **102** | On my heart imprint your image |
| 23:42 | **309** | Lord Jesus, think on me |
| 23:43 | **112, 113 part II** | Jesus, in thy dying woes |
| 23:44-45 | **130** | Christ the Lord is ris'n today! |
| 23:44-46 | **98** | Alas! And did my Savior bleed |
| 23:46 | **P. 156** | Into your hands, O Lord (in Prayer at the Close of the Day) |
| | **97** | Christ, the life of all the living |
| | **112, 113 part VII** | Jesus, in thy dying woes |
| 23:46, 53 | **91** | Savior, when in dust to you |
| 23:53 | **92** | Were you there when they crucified my Lord? |
| 24:1 | **139** | O sons and daughters of the King |
| | **251 v2** | O day of rest and gladness |
| 24:1-8 | **P. 138f** | On the first day of the week at early dawn (the Paschal Blessing in Morning Prayer) |
| | **92** | Were you there when they crucified my Lord? |
| | **109** | Go to dark Gethsemane |
| | **130** | Christ the Lord is ris'n today! |
| | **137** | Christians, to the paschal victim |
| | **145** | Thine is the glory |
| | **151** | Jesus Christ is ris'n today |
| | **154** | That Easter day with joy was bright |
| | **170** | Crown him with many crowns |
| 24:28-35 | **209** | Come, risen Lord and deign to be our guest |
| 24:29 | **P. 142** | Jesus Christ is the light of the world (in the service of Light, Evening Prayer) |
| | **263** | Abide with us, our savior |
| | **272** | Abide with me, fast falls the eventide |
| 24:32 | **243** | Lord, with glowing heart I'd praise thee |
| 24:36 | **154** | That Easter day with joy was bright |
| 24:41 | **246** | The first day of the week |

## JOHN

| | | |
|---|---|---|
| 1:1-4 | **179** | At the name of Jesus |

JOHN (continued)

| | | |
|---|---|---|
| 1:1-4, 14 | 374 | We all believe in one true God |
| 1:1-5 | 49 | O Savior of our fallen race |
| | 233 | Thy strong word did cleave the darkness |
| 1:1-14 | 400 | God, whose almighty word |
| 1:4 | P. 142 | Jesus, light of the world (in the service of Light, Evening Prayer) |
| 1:7 | 198 | Let all mortal flesh keep silence |
| 1:9 | 77 | O one with God the Father |
| | 279 | Oh, gladsome Light of the Father immortal |
| 1:14 | 28 | Savior of the nations, come |
| | 48 | All praise to you, eternal Lord |
| | 57 v3 | Let our gladness have no end, Hallelujah! |
| | 73 | All hail to you, O blessed morn! |
| | 83 | From God the Father, virgin-born |
| | 90 | Songs of thankfulness and praise |
| | 231 | O Word of God incarnate |
| | 271 | O Splendor of the Father's light |
| | 522 | Come, thou almighty King |
| 1:16 | 185 | Great God, a blessing from your throne |
| | 265 | Christ, whose glory fills the skies |
| | 497 | I heard the voice of Jesus say |
| 1:29, 35-36 | P. 72, 92, 103 114 | Lamb of God (in the orders for Holy Communion) |
| | Cant. 1 | Jesus, Lamb of God |
| | 103 | O Christ, thou Lamp of God |
| | 111 | Lamb of God, pure and sinless |
| | 296 | Just as I am, without one plea |
| | 305 | I lay my sins on Jesus |
| 1:35-36 | 37 | Hark! A thrilling voice is sounding! |
| 1:35-39 | 506 | Dear Lord and Father of mankind |
| 1:40 | 494 | Jesus calls us; o'er the tumult |
| 1:40-42 | 177 v5 | By all your saints in warfare |
| 1:40-51 | 178 v14 | By all your saints in warfare |
| 2:1-11 | 78 | All praise to you, O Lord |
| | 85 | When Christ's appearing was made known |
| | 90 | Songs of thankfulness and praise |
| 3:16 | 292 | God loved the world so that he gave |
| 4:13ff | 497 v2 | I heard the voice of Jesus say |
| 4:35-38 | 407 | Come, you thankful people, come |
| 4:42 | 420 | Lord, save your world; in bitter need |
| | 518 | Beautiful Savior |

JOHN (continued)

| | | |
|---|---|---|
| Ch. 6 | 487 | Let us ever walk with Jesus |
| 6:5-14 | 235 v2 | Break now the bread of life |
| 6:16-21 | 334 | Jesus, Savior, pilot me |
| | 467 | Eternal Father, strong to save |
| 6:28-35 | 392 | O Lord, send forth your Spirit |
| 6:33 | 343 v1 | Guide me ever, great Redeemer |
| 6:35 | 197 | O Living Bread from heaven |
| | 211 | Here, O my Lord, I see thee face to face |
| | 222 | O Bread of life from heaven |
| | 224 | Soul, adorn yourself with gladness |
| | 414 | O God of love, O King of peace |
| | 497 v2 | I heard the voice of Jesus say |
| 6:37 | 291 | Jesus sinners will receive |
| | 296 | Just as I am, without one plea |
| | 414 | O God of love, O King of peace |
| 6:41 | 197 | O living Bread from heaven |
| | 356 | O Jesus, joy of loving hearts |
| 6:48-51 | 222 | O Bread of life from heaven |
| 6:51 | 197 | O living Bread from heaven |
| | 207 | We who once were dead |
| | 224 | Soul, adorn yourself with gladness |
| | 356 | O Jesus, joy of loving hearts |
| 6:51-55 | 223 | In the quiet consecration |
| 6:68 | P. 62, 83, 103 | Alleluia, Lord, to whom shall we go (in the Orders for Holy Communion) |
| 7:37 | 497 v2 | I heard the voice of Jesus say |
| 8:1 | 324 | O Love that will not let me go |
| 8:12 | 75 | Bright and glorious is the sky |
| | 77 | O one with God the Father |
| | 249 | God himself is present |
| | 271 | O splendor of the Father's light |
| | 273 | O Christ, you are the light and day |
| | 356 | O Jesus, joy of loving hearts |
| | 455 | "Come, follow me," the Savior spake |
| | 497 | I heard the voice of Jesus say |
| 8:31 | 230 | Lord, keep us steadfast in your Word |
| 8:31b-32 | 248 | Dearest Jesus, at your word |
| 8:36 | 372 | In Adam we have all been one |
| 9:4 | 436 | All who love and serve your city |
| 10:1-18, 25-28 | 371 | With God as our friend, with his Spirit and Word |
| | 372 | In Adam we have all been one |
| | 481 | Savior, like a shepherd lead us |
| | 451 | The Lord's my shepherd |
| | 456 | The King of love my shepherd is |

JOHN (continued)

| | | |
|---|---|---|
| 10:9 | **47** | Let all together praise our God |
| 10:11 | **123** | Ah, holy Jesus, how hast thou offended |
| | **290** | There's a wideness in God's mercy |
| | **336** | Jesus, thy boundless love to me |
| | **371** | With God as our friend, with his Spirit and Word |
| 10:14 | **372** | In Adam we have all been one |
| 10:14-16 | **196 v2** | Praise the Lord, rise up rejoicing |
| 10:27-30 | **468** | From God can nothing move me |
| 11:16 | **487** | Let us ever walk with Jesus |
| | **492** | O Master, let me walk with you |
| 11:25 | **100** | Deep were his wounds, and red |
| 11:35 | **73** | All hail to you, O blessed morn! |
| Ch. 12 | **377** | Lift high the cross, the love of Christ proclaim |
| 12:18 | **392** | O Lord, send forth your Spirit |
| 12:20-22 | **177 v5** | By all your saints in warfare |
| | **178 v14** | By all your saints in warfare |
| 12:24 | **148** | Now the green blade rises from the buried grain |
| 12:35, 36 | **487** | Let us ever walk with Jesus |
| | **492** | O Master, let me walk with you |
| 13:3-11 | **122** | Love consecrates the humblest act |
| 13:7 | **483** | God moves in a mysterious way |
| 14:1 | **469** | Lord of all hopefulness, Lord of all joy |
| 14:1-7 | **302** | Jesus, your blood and righteousness |
| | **352** | I know that my Redeemer lives! |
| | **477** | O God of Jacob by whose hand |
| 14:1ff | **267** | Father, we praise you, now the night is over |
| 14:2 | **352** | I know that my Redeemer lives! |
| 14:3 | **147** | Hallelujah! Jesus lives! |
| | **351** | Oh, happy day when we shall stand |
| 14:6 | **351** | Oh, happy day when we shall stand |
| | **464** | You are the way; through you alone |
| | **513** | Come, my way, my truth, my life |
| 14:8-14 | **178 v14** | By all your saints in warfare |
| 14:9-11 | **157** | A hymn of glory let us sing! |
| 14:15-18 | **325** | Lord, thee I love with all my heart |
| 14:16 | **166** | All glory be to God on high |
| | **478** | Come, oh, come, O quick'ning Spirit |
| | **508** | Come down, O love divine |
| 14:16-17 | **354** | Eternal God, before your throne we bend |
| 14:23 | **502** | Thee will I love, my strength, my tow'r |
| 14:26 | **472,** | |
| | **473 v4** | Come, Holy Ghost, our souls inspire |

## JOHN (continued)

| | | |
|---|---|---|
| 14:27 | 338 | Peace, to soothe our bitter woes |
| | 449 | They cast their nets in Galilee |
| Ch. 15 | 378 | Amid the world's bleak wilderness |
| 15:1-8 | 306 | Chief of sinners though I be |
| 15:5 | 178 | By all your saints in warfare |
| 15:9-14 | 422 | O God, empower us to stem |
| 15:11 | 356 | O Jesus, joy of loving hearts |
| 15:12 | 422 | O God, empower us to stem |
| 15:13-15 | 298 | One there is, above all others |
| 15:14-16 | 439 | What a friend we have in Jesus |
| 16:11, 24 | 552 | In thee is gladness |
| 16:13 | 163 | Come, Holy Ghost, God and Lord |
| | 257 | Holy Spirit, truth divine |
| | 317 | To God the Holy Spirit let us pray |
| | 392 | O Lord, send forth your Spirit |
| | 475 | Come, gracious Spirit, heavn'ly dove |
| | 508 | Come down, O Love divine |
| 16:13-15 | 284 | Creator Spirit, heavn'ly dove |
| Ch. 17 | 410 | We give thee but thine own |
| 17:11b-19 | 364 | Son of God, eternal Savior |
| | 369 | The church's one foundation |
| 17:17 | 376 | Your kingdom come! O Father, hear our prayer |
| 17:20-23 | 77 | O one with God the Father |
| | 88 | Oh, love, how deep, how broad, how high |
| | 206 | Lord, who the night you were betrayed did pray |
| | 255 | Lord, receive this company |
| | 372 | In Adam we have all been one |
| 17:23 | 364 | Son of God, eternal Savior |
| 18:11 | 183 | The Son of God goes forth to war |
| 18:56 | 495 | Lead on, O King eternal |
| Ch. 19 | 301 | Come to Calv'ry's holy mountain |
| 19:2 | 116,117 | O sacred head, now wounded |
| | 421 | Lord Christ, when first you came to earth |
| 19:17 | 106 | In the hour of trial |
| 19:25 | 110 | At the cross, her station keeping |
| 19:26-27 | 112,113 part III | Jesus, in thy dying woes |
| 19:28 | 112,113 part V | Jesus, in thy dying woes |
| 19:30 | 112,113 part VI | Jesus, in thy dying woes |
| 19:34 | 222 | O Bread of life from heaven |
| | 327 | Rock of Ages, cleft for me |

## JOHN (continued)

| | | |
|---|---|---|
| 19:37 | **27** | Lo! He comes with clouds descending |
| Ch. 20 | **139** (v5-8) | O sons and daughters of the King |
| 20:11-18 | **137** | Christians, to the paschal victim |
| 20:15 | **147** | Hallelujah! Jesus lives |
| 20:19 | **262** | Savior, again to your dear name we raise |
| | **338** | Peace, to soothe our bitter woes |
| 20:19-20, 27-28 | **131** | Christ is risen! Alleluia! |
| 20:19-23 | **246** | The first day of the week |
| 20:22 | **488** | Breathe on me, breath of God |
| 20:24ff | **139** | O sons and daughters of the king |
| | **325** | Lord, thee I love with all my heart |
| 20:26-28 | **177 v6** | By all your saints in warfare |
| 20:27-28 | **131** | Christ is risen! Alleluia! |
| Ch. 21 | **449** | They cast their nets in Galilee |
| 21:15-17 | **177 v10** | By all your saints in warfare |
| | **286** | Bow down your ear, almighty Lord |
| 21:19-24 | **470** | Praise and thanks and adoration |
| 21:20-25 | **177 v8** | By all your saints in warfare |

## ACTS

| | | |
|---|---|---|
| 1:9 | **142** | Hail thee, festival day! |
| 1:9-11 | **157** | A hymn of glory let us sing! |
| | **159** | Up through endless ranks of angels |
| | **391** | And have the bright immensities |
| 1:12-14 | **177 v12** | By all your saints on warfare |
| 1:21-26 | **177** | By all your saints in warfare |
| 2:1-3 | **142** | Hail thee, festival day! |
| 2:1-4 | **161** | O day of grace that now we see |
| | **162** | Lord God, the Holy Ghost |
| | **251** | O day of rest and gladness |
| | **387** | Spirit of God, unleashed on earth |
| | **388** | O Spirit of the living God |
| | **396** | O God, O Lord of heav'n and earth |
| 2:3 | **285** | Spirit of God, sent from heaven abroad |
| 2:4 | **163** | Come, Holy Ghost, God and Lord |
| 4:12 | **395** | I trust, O Christ, in you alone |
| 7:59-60 | **177 v7** | By all your saints in warfare |
| 8:39 | **260** | On our way rejoicing |
| 9:1-6 | **177 v11** | By all your saints in warfare |
| 9:21 | **448** | Amazing grace, how sweet the sound |
| 9:28ff | **283** | O God, send heralds who will never falter |
| 10:38 | **417** | In a lowly manger born |

ACTS (continued)

| | | |
|---|---|---|
| 12:1-2 | **178 v16** | By all your saints in warfare |
| 12:1-5 | **183** | The Son of God goes forth to war |
| 14:3 | **283** | O God, send heralds who will never falter |
| 16:31 | **460** | I am trusting you, Lord Jesus |
| 17:24 | **365** | Built on a rock the Church shall stand |
| 17:28 | **397** | O Zion, haste, your mission high fulfilling |
| 20:17-36 | **370** | Blest be the tie that binds |
| 20:35 | **424 v2** | Lord of glory, you have bought us |
| Ch. 27 | **467** | Eternal Father, strong to save |

## ROMANS

| | | |
|---|---|---|
| 1:16 | **389** | Stand up, stand up for Jesus |
| 3:21-28 | **297** | Salvation unto us has come |
| 3:22b-24 | **448** | Amazing grace, how sweet the sound |
| 3:28 | **299** | Dear Christians, one and all, rejoice |
| | **395** | I trust, O Christ, in you alone |
| Ch. 4 | **544** | The God of Abr'ham praise |
| Ch. 5 | **372** | In Adam we have all been one |
| 5:1-2 | **297** | Salvation unto us has come |
| 5:1-5 | **163** | Come, Holy Ghost, God and Lord |
| 5:8-11 | **306** | Chief of sinners though I be |
| 5:9 | **215** | O Lord, we praise you, bless you, and adore you |
| 5:12-21 | **372** | In Adam we have all been one |
| 5:20-21 | **295** | Out of the depths I cry to you |
| 6:1-11 | **P. 141** | The Paschal Blessing (in Morning Prayer) |
| | **192** | Baptized into your name most holy |
| | **194** | All who believe and are baptized |
| | **195** | This is the Spirit's entry now |
| 6:3-4 | **128** | Christ the Lord is ris'n today; Alleluia! |
| | **189** | We know that Christ is raised and dies no more |
| 6:9 | **128** | Christ the Lord is ris'n today; Alleluia! |
| 6:16 | **490** | Let me be yours forever |
| Ch. 8 | **324** | O Love that will not let me go |
| 8:1-10 | **297** | Salvation unto us has come |
| 8:11ff | **133** | Jesus lives! The vict'ry's won! |
| 8:12-14 | **499** | Come, thou Fount of ev'ry blessing |
| 8:17 | **129** | Awake, my heart, with gladness |
| 8:18-23 | **493** | Hope of the world, thou Christ of great compassion |
| 8:19-21 | **272** | Abide with me, fast falls the eventide |

## ROMANS (continued)

| | | |
|---|---|---|
| 8:26-27 | **441** | Eternal Spirit of the living Christ |
| | **486** | Spirit of God, descend upon my heart |
| 8:28-30 | **446** | Whatever God ordains is right |
| | **447** | All depends on our possessing |
| 8:29 | **102** | On my heart imprint your image |
| | **537** | O Jesus, king most wonderful! |
| 8:31-39 | **340** | Jesus Christ, my sure defense |
| | **454** | If God himself be for me |
| | **552** | In thee is gladness |
| 8:32 | **379** | Spread, oh, spread, almighty Word |
| 8:34 | **158 v3** | Alleluia! Sing to Jesus |
| | **364** | Son of God, eternal Savior |
| | **395** | I trust, O Christ, in you alone |
| 8:35ff | **468** | From God can nothing move me |
| 8:37 | **145** | Thine is the glory |
| | **182 v2** | Rise, O children of salvation |
| 8:38 | **474** | Children of the heav'nly Father |
| Ch. 10 | **202** | Victim Divine, your grace we claim |
| 10:14-18 | **335** | May God bestow on us his grace |
| | **379** | Spread, oh, spread, almighty Word |
| 11:33, 36 | **Cant. 11** | Now listen, you servants of God |
| 12:1 | **98** | Alas! And did my Savior bleed |
| 12:3-8 | **381** | Hark, the voice of Jesus calling |
| 12:4-5 | **126** | Where charity and love prevail |
| | **255** | Lord, receive this company |
| 12:11 | **444** | With the Lord begin your task |
| 13:1-7 | **569** | God bless our native land |
| 13:11-12 | **37** | Hark! A thrilling voice is sounding |
| 14:8 | **399** | We are the Lord's. His all-sufficient merit |
| | **552** | In thee is gladness |
| 15:5 | **555** | When in our music God is glorified |
| 15:13 | **300** | O Christ, our hope, our heart's desire |
| | **469** | Lord of all hopefulness, Lord of all joy |
| | **493** | Hope of the world, thou Christ of great compassion |

## 1 CORINTHIANS

| | | |
|---|---|---|
| 1:9 | **504** | O God, my faithful God |
| 1:10-17 | **126** | Where charity and love prevail |
| 1:26-31 | **482** | When I survey the wondrous cross |
| 1:30 | **119** | Nature with open volume stands |
| | **297** | Salvation unto us has come |
| 2:1-5 | **377** | Lift high the cross, the love of Christ proclaim |
| 2:6-16 | **483** | God moves in a mysterious way |

1 CORINTHIANS (continued)

| | | |
|---|---|---|
| 2:9 | **31** | Wake, awake, for night is flying |
| | **330** | In heav'n above, in heav'n above |
| 2:14-16 | **523** | Holy Spirit, ever dwelling |
| 3:6 | **261** | On what has now been sown |
| 3:11 | **365** | Built on a rock the Church shall stand |
| | **367** | Christ is made the sure foundation |
| | **369** | The Church's one foundation |
| | **507** | How firm a foundation, O saints of the Lord |
| 3:16 | **164** | Creator Spirit, by whose aid |
| | **365** | Built on a rock the Church shall stand |
| | **375** | Only-begotten, Word of God eternal |
| | **459** | O Holy Spirit, enter in |
| 4:1-6 | **380** | O Christ, our light, O Radiance true |
| 5:7-8 | **Cant. 10** | Sing praise to the Lord |
| | **128** | Christ the Lord is ris'n today; Alleluia! |
| | **134** | Christ Jesus lay in death's strong bands |
| | **137** | Christians, to the paschal victim |
| | **172** | Lord, enthroned in heav'nly splendor |
| | **210** | At the Lamb's high feast we sing |
| 6:19-20 | **367** | Christ is made the sure foundation |
| 9:24 | **461** | Fight the good fight with all your might |
| 10:3 | **343** | Guide me ever, great Redeemer |
| 10:4 | **327** | Rock of Ages, cleft for me |
| 10:12-13 | **341** | Jesus, still lead on |
| | **485** | Lord, as a pilgrim through life I go |
| 10:13 | **504** | O God, my faithful God |
| 10:16 | **226** | Draw near and take the body of the Lord |
| 10:16-17 | **203** | Now we join in celebration |
| | **204** | Cup of blessing that we share |
| | **209** | Come, risen Lord and deign to be our guest |
| | **212** | Let us break bread together on our knees |
| | **214** | Come, let us eat, for now the feast is spread |
| | **217** | We place upon your table, Lord |
| 10:17 | **206** | Lord, who the night you were betrayed did pray |
| | **225** | Lord Jesus Christ, we humbly pray |
| | **226** | Draw near and take the body of the Lord |
| 10:31 | **166** | All glory be to God on high |
| | **267** | Father, we praise you, now the night is over |
| | **269** | Awake, my soul, and with the sun |
| 11:23-26 | **120** | Of the glorious body telling |

## 1 CORINTHIANS (continued)

| | | |
|---|---|---|
| | 127 | It happened on that fateful night |
| | 208 | Lord Jesus Christ, you have prepared |
| | 496 | Around you, O Lord Jesus |
| 11:28 | 213 | I come, O Savior, to your table |
| Ch. 12 | 381 | Hark, the voice of Jesus calling |
| Ch. 13 | 508 | Come down, O Love divine |
| 15:10 | 448 | Amazing grace, how sweet the sound |
| 15:12-19 | 149 | This joyful Eastertide |
| 15:17-20 | 136 | Christ is arisen |
| 15:20 | 340 | Jesus Christ, my sure defense |
| 15:23-26 | 120 | Of the glorious body telling |
| 15:25 | 171 | Rejoice, the Lord is king! |
| | 389 | Stand up, stand up for Jesus |
| 15:31 | P. 141 | The Paschal Blessing (in Morning Prayer) |
| | 192 | Baptized into your name most holy |
| | 195 | This is the Spirit's entry now |
| | 350 | Even as we live each day |
| 15:35ff | 148 | Now the green blade rises from the buried grain |
| 15:49 | 537 | O Jesus, king most wonderful! |
| 15:51ff | 346 | When peace, like a river, attendeth my way |
| | 407 | Come, you thankful people, come |
| 15:52 | 321 | The day is surely drawing near |
| 15:55 | 96 | Your heart, O God is grieved, we know |
| | 134 | Christ Jesus lay in death's strong hands |
| | 145 | Thine is the glory |
| | 150 | Make songs of joy to Christ, our head |
| | 272 v4 | Abide with me, fast falls the eventide |
| 15:54-56 | 139 | O sons and daughters of the King |
| 15:55-57 | 130 | Christ the Lord is ris'n today! |
| | 135 | The strife is o'er, the battle done |
| 15:57 | 138 | He is arisen! Glorious Word! |
| | 139 | O sons and daughters of the King |
| | 140 | With high delight let us unite |
| | 493 | Hope of the world, thou Christ of great compassion |
| 16:13 | 389 | Stand up, stand up for Jesus |
| 16:22 | 394 | Lost in the night do the people yet languish |

## 2 CORINTHIANS

| | | |
|---|---|---|
| 1:3-4 | 240 | Father of mercies, in your Word |
| 3:18 | 102 | On my heart imprint your image |
| | 315 | Love divine, all loves excelling |

## 2 CORINTHIANS (continued)

| | | |
|---|---|---|
| | 511 | Renew me, O eternal Light |
| 4:6 | P. 142 | Jesus, Light of the world (in the Service of Light, Evening Prayer) |
| | 233 | Thy strong word did cleave the darkness |
| | 400 | God, whose almighty word |
| 4:7 | 457 | Jesus, priceless treasure |
| 4:7-12 | 447 | All depends on our possessing |
| 5:17 | 189 | We know that Christ is raised and dies no more |
| | 194 | All who believe and are baptized |
| 5:19 | 60 | Hark! The herald angels sing |
| 6:1 | 434 | The Son of God, our Christ, the Word, the Way |
| | 444 | With the Lord begin your task |
| 6:2 | 181 | Greet now the swiftly changing year |
| 6:16 | 250 v2 | Open now thy gates of beauty |
| | 365 | Built on a rock the Church shall stand |
| 7:10 | 438 | Lord, teach us how to pray aright |
| 8:8-15 | 408 | God, whose giving knows no ending |
| 9:15 | 220 | O Jesus, blessed Lord, to you |
| 13:14 | 288 | Hear us now, our God and Father |

## GALATIANS

| | | |
|---|---|---|
| 1:1 | 142 | Hail thee, festival day! |
| 1:11-24 | 177 v11 | By all your saints in warfare |
| 2:20 | 94 | My song is love unknown |
| | 336 | Jesus, thy boundless love to me |
| | 406 | Take my life, that I may be |
| 2:22 | 390 | I love to tell the story |
| Ch. 3 | 544 | The God of Abr'ham praise |
| 3:13 | 118 | Sing, my tongue, the glorious battle |
| 4:26 | 348 | Jerusalem, whose towers touch the skies |
| 5:13-25 | 486 | Spirit of God, descend upon my heart |
| 5:22 | 284 | O perfect love, all human thought transcending |
| Ch. 6 | 395 v3 | I trust Christ, in you alone |
| 6:1-10, 14-16 | 402 | Look from your sphere of endless day |
| 6:2 | 370 | Blest be the tie that binds |
| | 395 | I trust, O Christ, in you alone |
| 6:14 | 140 | In the cross of Christ I glory |
| | 107 | Beneath the cross of Jesus |
| | 173 | The head that once was crowned with thorns |

GALATIANS (continued)

|  |  |  |
|---|---|---|
|  | 344 | We sing the praise of him who died |
|  | 482 | When I survey the wondrous cross |

**EPHESIANS**

| | | |
|---|---|---|
| 1:9 | 483 | God moves in a mysterious way |
| 1:1-14 | 396 | O God, O Lord of heav'n and earth |
| 1:23 | 265 | Christ, whose glory fills the skies |
| 2:1 | 100 | Deep were his wounds, and red |
|  | 207 | We who once were dead |
| 2:4-8 | 448 | Amazing grace, how sweet the sound |
| 2:4-10 | 297 | Salvation unto us has come |
| 2:13-22 | 255 | Lord, receive this company |
| 2:19-22 | 365 | Built on a rock the Church shall stand |
|  | 367 | Christ is made the sure foundation |
| 2:20 | 369 | The Church's one foundation |
| 2:20-22 | 446 | Whatever God ordains is right |
| 3:7-9 | 523 | Holy Spirit, ever dwelling |
| 3:14-19 | 88 | Oh, love, how deep, how broad, how high |
|  | 290 | There's a wideness in God's mercy |
|  | 401 | Before you, Lord, we bow |
| 3:19 | 265 | Christ, whose glory fills the skies |
| 4:1-7 | 425 | O God of mercy, God of light |
| 4:3-4 | 369 | The Church's one foundation |
| 4:3-6 | 370 | Blest be the tie that binds |
| 4:4-6 | 191 | Praise and thanksgiving be to God our maker |
|  | 509 | Onward, Christian soldiers |
|  | 160 | Filled with the Spirit's power, with one accord |
| 4:5 | 355 | Through the night of doubt and sorrow |
| 4:6 | 373 | Eternal Ruler of the ceaseless round |
| 4:11-13 | 408 | God, whose giving knows no ending |
| 4:12 | 433 | The Church of Christ, in every age |
| 4:15-16 | 414 | O God of love, O King of peace |
| 4:17-24 | 504 | O God, my faithful God |
|  | 511 | Renew me, O eternal Light |
| 4:22 | 22 | The advent of our God |
| 4:24 | 537 | O Jesus, king most wonderful |
| 4:30 | 96 | Your heart, O God, is grieved, we know |
| Ch. 5 | 369 | The Church's one foundation |
| 5:2 | 487 | Let us ever walk with Jesus |
|  | 492 | O Master, let me walk with you |
| 5:8-14 | 396 | O God, O Lord of Heav'n and earth |
| 5:14 | 129 | Awake, my heart, with gladness |
|  | 269 | Awake, my soul and with the sun |

## EPHESIANS (continued)

| | | |
|---|---|---|
| 5:18-20 | 555 | When in our music God is glorified |
| | 557 | Let all things now living |
| 5:21-6:4 | 357 | Our father, by whose name |
| | 512 | Oh, blest the house whate'er befall |
| 6:4 | 440 | Christians, while on earth abiding |
| 6:5-9 | 444 | With the Lord begin your task |
| 6:10 | 509 | Onward, Christian Soldiers |
| 6:10-11 | 373 | Eternal Ruler of the ceaseless round |
| 6:10-20 | 188 | I bind unto myself today |
| | 308 | God the Father, be our stay |
| | 366 | Lord of our life, and God of our salvation |
| | 373 | Eternal Ruler of the ceaseless round |
| | 437 | Not alone for mighty empire |
| 6:11-17 | 389 | Stand up, stand up for Jesus |
| 6:16 | 273 | O Christ, you are the light and day |
| 6:19ff | 283 | O God, send heralds who will never falter |
| 6:24 | 406 | Take my life that I may be |

## PHILIPPIANS

| | | |
|---|---|---|
| 1:10-21 | 419 | Lord of all nations, grant me grace |
| 1:21 | 176 | For all your saints, O Lord |
| | 399 | We are the Lord's. His all-sufficient merit |
| | 489 | Wide open are your hands |
| 1:27 | 160 | Filled with the Spirit's pow'r, with one accord |
| 1:29 | 173 | The head that once was crowned with thorns |
| Ch. 2 | 83 | From God the Father, virgin-born |
| 2:1-18 | 419 | Lord of all nations, grant me grace |
| 2:5-7 | 64 | From east to west, from shore to shore |
| 2:5-11 | Cant. 20 | Christ Jesus being in the form of God |
| | 179 | At the name of Jesus |
| | 377 | Lift high the cross |
| 2:7 | 22 | The advent of our God |
| 2:9 | 514 | O Savior, precious Savior |
| 2:9-11 | 156 v1 | Look, oh look, the sight is glorious |
| | 401 | Before you, Lord, we bow |
| | 545 | When morning gilds the skies |
| 2:10-11 | 388 | O Spirit of the living God |
| | 537 | O Jesus, king most wonderful |
| 3:7-11 | 482 | When I survey the wondrous cross |
| 3:8 | 344 | We sing the praise of him who died |
| 3:9 | 293, 294 | My hope if built on nothing less |

## PHILIPPIANS (continued)

| | | |
|---|---|---|
| 4:4 | 299 | Dear Christians, one and all, rejoice |
| | 552 | In thee is gladness |
| | 553 | Rejoice, O pilgrim throng! |
| 4:7 | 449 | They cast their nets in Galilee |

## COLOSSIANS

| | | |
|---|---|---|
| 1:13-20 | 42 | Of the Father's love begotten |
| 1:15-20 | 152 | Look, how he stands |
| | 391 | And have the bright immensities |
| 1:24 | 421 | Lord Christ, when first you came to earth |
| | 424 | Lord of glory, you have bought us |
| 2:3 | 457 | Jesus, priceless treasure |
| 2:13-15 | 207 | We who once were dead |
| 2:14 | 326 | My heart is longing to praise my savior |
| 2:15 | 129 | Awake, my heart, with gladness |
| Ch. 3 | 302 | Jesus, your blood and righteousness |
| 3:1 | 157 | A hymn of glory let us sing! |
| 3:1-4 | 511 | Renew me, O eternal Light |
| 3:8-11 | 373 | Eternal Ruler of the ceaseless round |
| 3:9ff | 537 | O Jesus, king most wonderful |
| 3:11 | 359 | In Christ there is no east or west |
| 3:16 | 555 | When in our music God is glorified |
| 3:17 | 444 | With the Lord begin your task |
| | 504 | O God, my faithful God |
| | 505 | Forth in thy name, O Lord, I go |
| 3:23-24 | 444 | With the Lord begin your task |

## 1 THESSALONIANS

| | | |
|---|---|---|
| 4:14 | 342 | I know of a sleep in Jesus' name |
| 4:15-18 | 321 | The day is surely drawing near |
| 4:16 | 346 | When peace, like a river, attendeth my way |
| 5:1-11 | 399 | We are the Lord's, His all-sufficient merit |
| | 443 | Rise, my soul, to watch and pray |
| 5:8 | 188 | I bind unto myself today |
| 5:23 | 257 | Holy Spirit, truth divine |

## 2 THESSALONIANS

| | | |
|---|---|---|
| 2:3 | 263 | Abide with us, our Savior |
| 3:1 | 382 | Awake, O Spirit of the watchmen |

## 2 THESSALONIANS (continued)

| | | |
|---|---|---|
| 3:3 | **504** | O God, my faithful God |
| 3:16 | **471** | Grant peace, we pray, in mercy, Lord |

## 1 TIMOTHY

| | | |
|---|---|---|
| 1:1 | **293, 294** | My hope is built on nothing less |
| 1:5 | **306** | Chief of sinners though I be |
| 1:14 | **448** | Amazing grace, how sweet the sound |
| 1:17 | **526** | Immortal, invisible, God only wise |
| 1:18 | **509** | Onward, Christian soldiers |
| 2:6 | **24** | Come, O precious Ransom, come |
| 3:16 | **42** | Of the Father's love begotten |
| 6:12 | **174** | For all the saints who from their labors rest |
| | **183** | The Son of God goes forth to war |
| | **461** | Fight the good fight |
| 6:16 | **516** | Arise, my soul, arise! |
| | **165 v3** | Holy, holy, holy, Lord God almighty! |
| 6:17-19 | **447** | All depends on our possessing |

## 2 TIMOTHY

| | | |
|---|---|---|
| 1:6-7 | **387** | Spirit of God, unleashed on earth |
| 1:7 | **257** | Holy Spirit, truth divine |
| 1:8-14 | **230** | Lord, keep us steadfast in your Word |
| | **487** | Let us ever walk with Jesus |
| 2:8-13 | **183** | The Son of God goes forth to war |
| | **487** | Let us ever walk with Jesus |
| | **500** | Faith of our fathers, living still |
| 2:11-12 | **Cant. 13** | Keep in mind that Jesus Christ has died for us |
| 2:19 | **507** | How firm a foundation, O saints of the Lord |
| 3:14—4:5 | **227** | How blest are they who hear God's Word |
| 4:6-8, 16-18 | **461** | Fight the good fight with all your might |

## TITUS

| | | |
|---|---|---|
| 1:9 | **239** | God's word is our great heritage |
| 3:5 | **387** | Spirit of God, unleashed on earth |

## HEBREWS

| | | |
|---|---|---|
| 1:1-2 | **238** | God has spoken by his prophets |
| 1:2 | **300** | O Christ, our hope, our hearts' desire |
| 1:3 | **171** | Rejoice, the Lord is king |

## HEBREWS (Continued)

| | | |
|---|---|---|
| 2:5 | **88** | Oh, love, how deep, how broad, how high |
| 2:9 | **156** | Look, oh look, the sight is glorious |
| | **170** | Crown him with many crowns |
| | **328, 329** | All hail the pow'r of Jesus' name |
| | **516** | Arise, my soul, arise! |
| 2:20 | **506** | Dear Lord and Father of mankind |
| 4:9 | **251** | O day of rest and gladness |
| | **315** | Love divine, all loves excelling |
| | **341** | Jesus, still lead on |
| 4:12 | **232** | Your word, O Lord, is gentle dew |
| 6:4ff | **516** | Arise, my soul, arise |
| 6:5 | **211** | Here, O my Lord, I see thee face to face |
| 6:6 | **115 v4** | Jesus, I will ponder now |
| | **419 v3** | Lord of all nations, grant me grace |
| 6:19 | **293, 294** | My hope is built on nothing less |
| 7:25 | **352** | I know that my Redeemer lives! |
| | **364** | Son of God, eternal Savior |
| 9:11-12 | **202 v2** | Victim Divine, your grace we claim |
| 9:14 | **155** | Praise the Savior, now and ever |
| 10:35 | **467** | Eternal Father, strong to save |
| 11:1 | **201** | O God of life's great mystery |
| 11:8-9 | **544** | The God of Abraham praise |
| 11:8-16 | **343** | Guide me ever, great Redeemer |
| | **485** | Lord as a pilgrim through life I go |
| | **498** | All who would valiant be |
| 12:1ff | **308** | God the Father, be our stay |
| 12:12 | **484** | God, my Lord, my strength, my place of hiding |
| 12:14 | **475** | Come, gracious Spirit, heav'nly dove |
| 12:22ff | **175** | Ye watchers and ye holy ones |
| 12:24 | **95** | Glory be to Jesus |
| | **302** | Jesus, your blood and righteousness |
| 13:1-3 | **419** | Lord of all nations, grant me grace |
| 13:5 | **453** | If you but trust in God to guide you |
| | **485** | Lord, as a pilgrim through life I go |
| 13:15 | **269** | Awake, my soul, and with the sun |
| | **561** | For the beauty of the earth |
| 13:20-21 | **481** | Savior, like a shepherd lead us |

## JAMES

| | | |
|---|---|---|
| 1:5 | **415** | God of grace and God of glory |
| 1:16 | **411** | Lord of all good, our gifts we bring you now |

## JAMES (continued)

| | | |
|---|---|---|
| 1:17 | 362 | We plow the fields and scatter |
| 1:17-27 | 480 | Oh, that the Lord would guide my ways |
| | 540 | O God, my faithful God |
| 1:27 | 410 | We give thee but thine own |
| 2:14-18 | 429 | Where cross the crowded ways of life |
| 3:13-18 | 126 | Where charity and love prevail |
| 4:1-2 | 414 | O God of love, O king of peace |
| 5:8 | 318 | The Lord will come and not be slow |
| 5:14f | 360 | O Christ, the healer, we have come |
| 5:16 | 126 | Where charity and love prevail |

## 1 PETER

| | | |
|---|---|---|
| 1:8 | 199 | Thee we adore, O hidden Savior |
| | 514 | O Savior, precious Savior |
| 1:17 | 343 | Guide me ever, great Redeemer |
| | 485 | Lord, as a pilgrim through life I go |
| | 498 | All who would valiant be |
| 1:18 | 165 v3 | Holy, holy, holy, Lord God Almighty |
| 1:18-19 | 369 | The Church's one foundation |
| | 457, 458 | Jesus, priceless treasure |
| 1:19 | 95 | Glory be to Jesus |
| 2:5 | 365 v3 | Built on a rock the Church shall stand |
| 2:7a | 537 | O Jesus, king most wonderful! |
| 2:7 | 367 | Christ is made the sure foundation |
| 2:21 | 487 | Let us ever walk with Jesus |
| 2:24 | 98 | Alas! And did my Savior bleed |
| | 100 | Deep were his wounds, and red |
| | 118 | Sing, my tongue, the glorious battle |
| | 300 | O Christ, our hope, our hearts' desire |
| | 395 | I trust, O Christ, in you alone |
| 2:25 | 243 | Lord, with glowing heart I'd praise thee |
| | 503 | O Jesus, I have promised |
| | 517 | Praise to the Father for his loving kindness |
| 3:18-19 | 153 | "Welcome, happy morning!" age to age shall say |
| 4:10 | 410 | We give thee but thine own |
| 5:2 | 286 | Bow down your ear, almighty Lord |
| 5:7 | 106 | In the hour of trial |
| | 461 | Fight the good fight with all your might |
| 5:8 | 228, 229 | A mighty fortress is our God |
| | 322 v1 | The clouds of judgment gather |
| 5:10 | Cant. 12 | God, who has called you to glory |

## 1 PETER (continued)

|  |  |  |
|---|---|---|
|  | **326** | My heart is longing to praise my Savior |

## 2 PETER

| 1:19 | **76** | O Morning Star, how fair and bright! |
|---|---|---|
|  | **233** | Thy strong word did cleave the darkness |
|  | **265** | Christ, whose glory fills the skies |
| 3:8-14 | **25** | Rejoice, rejoice, believers |
|  | **243** | Lord, with glowing heart I'd praise thee |
|  | **320** | O God, our help in ages past |
| 3:9 | **3138** | The Lord will come and not be slow |

## 1 JOHN

| 1:7 | **199** | Thee we adore, O hidden Savior |
|---|---|---|
|  | **211** | Here, O my Lord, I see thee face to face |
|  | **293,** |  |
|  | **294** | My hope is built on nothing less |
|  | **559** | Oh, for a thousand tongues to sing |
| 1:15 | **526** | Immortal, invisible, God only wise |
| 2:6 | **492** | O Master, let me walk with you |
| 3:17-18 | **410** | We give thee but thine own |
| 4:8 | **344** | We sing the praise of him who died |
| 5:6-9 | **327** | Rock of Ages, cleft for me |

## REVELATION

| 1:5-6 | **167** | Glory be to God the Father! |
|---|---|---|
| 1:8, 18 | **42** | Of the Father's love begotten |
| 1:9-10 | **177 v8** | By all your saints in warfare |
| 1:10 | **246** | The first day of the week |
| 1:18 | **151** | Jesus Christ is ris'n today |
| 1:20 | **231** | O word of God incarnate |
| 2:10 | **174** | For all the saints who from their labors rest |
|  | **459** | O Holy Spirit, enter in |
| 2:7ff | **377** | Lift high the cross, the love of Christ proclaim |
| 2:10 | **490** | Let me be yours forever |
| 2:10b | **389** | Stand up, stand up for Jesus |
| 3:7 | **34** | Oh, come, oh, come, Emmanuel |
| 3:8 | **304** | Today your mercy calls us |
| 3:17 | **296** | Just as I am, without one plea |
| 4:8 | **432** | We worship you, O God of might |
| 4:8-11 | **165** | Holy, holy, holy, Lord God Almighty |
| 4:10-11 | **315 v4** | Love divine, all loves excelling |
| 4:11 | **37** | Hark! A thrilling voice is sounding! |

## REVELATION (continued)

| | | |
|---|---|---|
| | 42 | Of the Father's love begotten |
| Ch. 5 | 536 | O God of God, O Light of Light |
| 5:9 | 24 | Come, O precious Ransom, come |
| | 158 | Alleluia! Sing to Jesus |
| | 558 | Earth and all stars! |
| 5:9-10 | 25 | Rejoice, rejoice, believers |
| 5:9-12 | P. 60, 81, 102 | This is the feast of victory for our God (from Holy Communion settings) |
| 5:9-16 | 328, 329 | All hail the pow'r of Jesus' name! |
| 5:11-12 | 354 | Eternal God, before your throne we bend |
| | 390 | I love to tell the story |
| 5:12 | 167 | Glory be to God the Father! |
| | 252 | You servants of God, your master proclaim |
| | 254 | Come, let us join our cheerful songs |
| | 344 | We sing the praise of him who died |
| | 525 | Blessing and honor and glory and pow'r |
| 5:12-13 | P. 60, 81, 102 | Worthy is Christ (from Holy Communion settings) |
| 5:13 | 432 | We worship you, O God of might |
| 5:19 | 24 | Come, O precious Ransom, come |
| 6:9-11 | 369 | The Church's one foundation |
| Ch. 7 | 525 | Blessing and honor and glory and pow'r |
| 7:3 | 182 v3 | Rise, O children of salvation |
| 7:9-12 | P. 60, 81, 102 | This is the feast of victory for our God (from Holy Communion settings) |
| | 175 | Ye watchers and ye holy ones |
| | 254 | Come, let us join our cheerful songs |
| | 348 | Jerusalem, whose towers touch the skies |
| | 535 | Holy God, we praise your name |
| 7:9-17 | 177 v4 | By all your saints in warfare |
| 7:10, 12 | P. 60, 81, 102 | Worthy is Christ (from Holy Communion settings) |
| 7:11-12 | 516 | Arise, my soul, arise! |
| 7:12 | 525 | Blessing and honor and glory and pow'r |
| 7:13-17 | 176 | For all your saints, O Lord |
| | 314 | Who is this host arrayed in white |
| 7:14 | 167 | Glory be to God the Father! |
| | 304 | Today your mercy calls us |
| | 305 | I lay my sins on Jesus |

REVELATION (continued)

| | | |
|---|---|---|
| | 516 | Arise, my soul, arise! |
| 7:15 | 315 v3 | Love divine, all loves excelling |
| 8:1-6 | 556 | Herald, sound the note of judgment |
| 14:13 | 174 | For all the saints who from their labors rest |
| | 342 | I know of a sleep in Jesus' name |
| 15:3-4 | Cant. 21 | O ruler of the universe, Lord God (Magna Et Mirabilia) |
| 17:14 | 383 | Rise up, O saints of God! |
| | 418 | Judge eternal, throned in splendor |
| 19:4, 6-9 | P. 60, 81, 102 | Worthy is Christ (from Holy Communion settings) |
| 19:6 | 171 | Rejoice, the Lord is king |
| 19:6-9 | 31 | Wake, awake, for night is flying |
| 19:7-10 | 78 | All praise to you, O Lord |
| 19:8 | 224 | Soul, adorn yourself with gladness |
| 19:11-14 | 183 | The Son of God goes forth to war |
| 19:11-16 | 108 | All glory, laud, and honor |
| 19:16 | 156 | Look, oh look, the sight is glorious |
| | 173 | The head that once was crowned with thorns |
| | 328, 329 | All hail the pow'r of Jesus' name |
| | 418 | Judge eternal, throned in splendor |
| 20:21 | 25 | Rejoice, rejoice, believers |
| 21:1-4 | 330 | In heav'n above, in heav'n above |
| | 331 | Jerusalem, my happy home |
| | 347 | Jerusalem the golden |
| 21:2-3 | 348 | Jerusalem, whose towers touch the skies |
| 21:2-4 | 337 | Oh, what their joy and their glory must be |
| 21:3-4 | 25 | Rejoice, rejoice, believers |
| 21:4 | 479 | My faith looks up to thee |
| 21:6 | 499 | Come, thou Fount of ev'ry blessing |
| 21:18-23 | 347 | Jerusalem the golden |
| 21:21 | 174 | For all the saints who from their labors rest |
| 21:21-22 | 31 | Wake, awake, for night is flying |
| 21:23 | 82 | As with gladness men of old |
| | 526 | Immortal, invisible, God only wise |
| 22:2 | 331 | Jerusalem, my happy home |
| 22:5 | 567 | God of our fathers, whose almight hand |
| 22:16 | 34 | Oh, come, oh, come, Emmanuel |
| | 38 | O Savior, rend the heavens wide |
| | 76 | O Morning Star, how fair and bright! |

## REVELATION (continued)

|  |  |  |
|---|---|---|
|  | 86 | The only Son from heaven |
| 22:17 | 224 | Soul, adorn yourself with gladness |
|  | 296 | Just as I am, without one plea |
| 22:20 | 33 | The King shall come when morning dawns |
|  | 394 | Lost in the night do the people yet languish |
|  | 407 | Come, you thankful people, come |

## THE CREED

374  We all believe in one true God

## THE TE DEUM

| P. 139 | Te Deum (in the service of Morning Prayer) |
|---|---|
| Cant. 3 | You are God; we praise you |
| 535 | Holy God, we praise your name |
| 547 | Thee we adore, eternal Lord |

## THE GREAT-O-ANTIPHONS

| PP. 174, 175 | (propers for Daily Prayer) |
|---|---|
| 34 | Oh, come, oh, come, Emmanuel |

## ST. PATRICK'S BREASTPLATE

188  I bind unto myself today

## ST. FRANCIS OF ASSISI'S CANTICLE OF THE SUN

527  All creatures of our God and King

## JOHN BUNYAN'S *PILGRIM'S PROGRESS*

498  All who would valiant be

II

**TOPICAL INDEX TO HYMNS**

## ADORATION

*See Praise, Adoration*

## ADVENT

*See 22-38*

| | |
|---|---|
| 6 | My soul proclaims the greatness of the Lord |
| 74 | A stable lamp is lighted |
| 76 | O Morning Star, how fair and bright |
| 86 | The only Son from heaven |
| 172 | Lord, enthroned in heavenly splendor |
| 180 | My soul now magnifies the Lord |
| 258 | Hosanna to the living Lord |
| 312 | Once he came in blessing |
| 321 | The day is surely drawing near |
| 322 | The clouds of judgment gather |
| 323 | O Lord of light, who made the stars |
| 351 | Oh, happy day when we shall stand |
| 355 | Through the night of doubt and sorrow |
| 394 | Lost in the night do the people yet languish |
| 397 | O Zion, haste, your mission high fulfilling |
| 400 | God, whose almighty word |
| 421 | Lord Christ, when first you came to earth |
| 529 | Praise God, from whom all blessings flow |
| 536 | O God of God, O Light of Light |
| 537 | O Jesus, king most wonderful |
| 556 | Herald, sound the note of judgment |

## AFFIRMATION OF BAPTISM

| | |
|---|---|
| 192 | Baptized into your name most holy |
| 333 | Lord, take my hand and lead me |
| 354 | Eternal God, before your throne we bend |
| 387 | Spirit of God, unleashed on earth |
| 455 | "Come, follow me", the Savior spake |
| 475 | Come, gracious Spirit, heav'nly dove |
| 478 | Come, oh, come, O quick'ning Spirit |

*See Commitment; Pentecost*

## AFFLICTION

*See Comfort and Rest*

## ALL SAINTS' DAY

| | |
|---|---|
| 174 | For all the saints who from their labors rest |
| 176 | For all your saints, O Lord |
| 245 | All people that on earth do dwell |
| 314 | Who is this host arrayed in white |
| 337 | Oh, what their joy and their glory must be |
| 351 | Oh, happy day when we shall stand |
| 500 | Faith of our fathers, living still |
| 564, 565 | Praise God, from whom all blessings flow |

## ANGELS

| | |
|---|---|
| 175 | Ye watchers and ye holy ones |
| 249 | God himself is present |
| 535 | Holy God, we praise your name |
| | See Christmas |

## ANNIVERSARY, CHURCH

| | |
|---|---|
| 163 | Come Holy Ghost, God and Lord |
| 169 | Father most holy, merciful, and tender |
| 182 | Rise, O children of salvation |
| 186 | How blessed is this place, O Lord |
| 320 | O God, our help in ages past |
| 365 | Built on a rock the Church shall stand |
| 367 | Christ is made the sure foundation |
| 369 | The Church's one foundation |
| 375 | Only-begotten, Word of God eternal |
| 440 | Christians, while on earth abiding |
| 472, 473 | Come, Holy Ghost, our souls inspire |
| 500 | Faith of our fathers |
| 512 | Oh, blest the house, whate'er befall |
| 523 | Holy Spirit, ever dwelling |
| 533, 534 | Now thank we all our God |
| 567 | God of our fathers, whose almighty hand |

## ANNUNCIATION OF OUR LORD, THE

| | |
|---|---|
| 42 | Of the Father's love begotten |
| 64 | From east to west, from shore to shore |
| 86 | The only Son from heaven |
| 180 | My soul now magnifies the Lord |

## ARTS AND MUSIC

| | |
|---|---|
| Cant. 10 | Sing praise to the Lord |
| 140 | With high delight let us unite |
| 144 | Good Christian friends, rejoice and sing |
| 146 | Rejoice, angelic choirs, rejoice |
| 216 v3 | For perfect love so freely spent |
| 253 v2 | Lord Jesus Christ, be present now |
| 385 v4 | What wondrous love is this, O my soul, O my soul |
| 390 | I love to tell the story |
| 406 v3 | Take my life, that I may be |
| 538 | Oh, praise the Lord, my soul |
| 539 v1 | Praise the Almighty, my soul adore him |
| 542 | Sing praise to God, the highest good |
| 553 | Rejoice, O pilgrim throng |
| 555 | When in our music God is glorified |
| 557 | Let all things now living |
| 558 | Earth and all stars |
| 559 | Oh, for a thousand tongues to sing |
| 560 | Oh, that I had a thousand voices |

## ASCENSION

| | |
|---|---|
| | see 156-159 |
| 142 | Hail thee, festival day |
| 170 | Crown him with many crowns |
| 171 | Rejoice, the Lord is King |
| 172 | Lord, enthroned in heav'nly splendor |
| 179 | At the name of Jesus |
| 300 | O Christ, our hope, our heart's desire |
| 363 | Christ is alive! Let Christians sing |
| 391 | And have the bright immensities |
| 536 | O God of God, O Light of Light |

## ASH WEDNESDAY

| | |
|---|---|
| 91 | Savior, when in dust to you |
| 99 | O Lord, throughout these forty days |
| 115 | Jesus, I will ponder now |
| 295 | Out of the depths I cry to you |
| 301 | Come to Calv'ry's holy mountain |
| | See *Lent, Repentance, Forgiveness; Sorrow* |

## ASPIRATION

| | |
|---|---|
| 300 | O Christ, our hope, our hearts' desire |

## ASPIRATION (continued)

| | |
|---|---|
| 315 | Love divine, all loves excelling |
| 324 | O Love that will not let me go |
| 336 | Jesus, thy boundless love to me |
| 452 | As pants the hart for cooling streams |
| 464 | You are the way; through you alone |

## ASSURANCE

| | |
|---|---|
| 290 | There's a wideness in God's mercy |
| 439 | What a friend we have in Jesus |
| 457, 458 | Jesus, priceless treasure |
| 497 | I heard the voice of Jesus say |
| 539 | Praise the Almighty, my soul, adore him |

*see Trust, Guidance*

## ATONEMENT

| | |
|---|---|
| 93 | Jesus, refuge of the weary |
| 94 | My song is love unknown |
| 97 | Christ, the life of all the living |
| 202 | Victim Divine, your grace we claim |
| 290 | There's a wideness in God's mercy |
| 293 | My hope is built on nothing less |
| 302 | Jesus, your blood and righteousness |
| 310 | To you, omniscient Lord of all |
| 417 | In a lowly manger born |
| 482 | When I survey the wondrous cross |

*See Redeemer*

## BAPTISM, CHRISTIAN

*See Holy Baptism*

## BAPTISM OF OUR LORD, THE

| | |
|---|---|
| 36 | On Jordan's banks the Baptist's cry |
| 79 | To Jordan came the Christ, our Lord |
| 83 | From God the Father, virgin-born |
| 85 | When Christ's appearing was made known |
| 192 | Baptized into your name most holy |
| 198 | Let all mortal flesh keep silence |
| 475 | Come, gracious Spirit, heavenly dove |

## BEGINNING OF SERVICE

*See 241-257*

## BEGINNING OF SERVICE (continued)

| | |
|---|---|
| 35 | Hark, the glad sound! The Savior comes |
| 140 | With high delight let us unite |
| 143 | Now all the vault of heav'n resounds |
| 161 | O day full of grace that we now see |
| 162 | Lord God, the Holy Ghost |
| 163 | Come, Holy Ghost, God and Lord |
| 165 | Holy, holy, holy, Lord God Almighty |
| 166 | All Glory be to God on high |
| 169 | Father most holy, merciful, and tender |
| 170 | Crown him with many crowns |
| 171 | Rejoice, the Lord is king! |
| 182 | Rise, O children of salvation |
| 196 | Praise the Lord, rise up rejoicing |
| 201 | O God of life's great mystery |
| 205 | Now the silence |
| 210 | At the Lamb's high feast we sing |
| 269 | Awake, my soul, and with the sun |
| 270 | God of our life, all-glorious Lord |
| 299 | Dear Christians, one and all, rejoice |
| 304 | Today your mercy calls us |
| 328 | All hail the pow'r of Jesus' name |
| 367 | Christ is made the sure foundation |
| 368 | I love your kingdom, Lord |
| 369 | The Church's one foundation |
| 377 | Lift high the cross, the love of Christ proclaim |
| 389 | Stand up, stand up for Jesus |
| 400 | God, whose almighty word |
| 401 | Before you, Lord, we bow |
| 415 | God of grace and God of glory |
| 427 | O Jesus Christ, may grateful hymns be rising |
| 443 | Rise, my soul, to watch and pray |
| 444 | With the Lord begin your task |
| 459 | O Holy Spirit, enter in |
| 473 | Come, Holy Ghost, our souls inspire |
| 478 | Come, oh, come, O quick'ning Spirit |
| 496 | Around you, O Lord Jesus |
| 511 | Renew me, O eternal Light |
| 516 | Arise, my soul, arise! |
| 519 | My soul, now praise your maker! |
| 520 | Give to our God immortal praise! |
| 521 | Let us with a gladsome mind |
| 522 | Come, thou almighty King |
| 525 | Blessing and honor and glory and pow'r |
| 530 | Jesus shall reign where'er the sun |
| 535 | Holy God, we praise your name |

## BEGINNING OF SERVICE (continued)

| | |
|---|---|
| 539 | Praise the Almighty, m;y soul, adore him! |
| 543 | Praise to the Lord, the Almighty, the King of creation! |
| 545, 546 | When morning gilds the skies |
| 548 | Oh, worship the King, all-glorious above |
| 549 | Praise, my soul, the King of heaven |
| 552 | In thee is gladness |
| 559 | Oh, for a thousand tongues to sing |
| 560 | Oh, that I had a thousand voices |
| 561 | For the beauty of the earth |

## BENEVOLENCE

See Stewardship; Offertory

## BIBLE

See Scriptures

## BURIAL

See Funeral

## CELEBRATION, JUBILATION

| | |
|---|---|
| | See 552-565 |
| 175 | Ye watchers and ye holy ones |
| 254 | Come, let us join our cheerful songs |
| 256 | Oh, sing jubilee to the Lord, ev'ry land |
| 315 | Love divine, all loves excelling |
| 328, 329 | All hail the pow'r of Jesus' name |
| 385 | What wondrous love is this, O my soul, O my soul! |

## CHRIST THE KING

| | |
|---|---|
| | See 170-173 |
| 33 | The King shall come when morning dawns |
| 179 | At the name of Jesus |
| 321 | The day is surely drawing near |
| 323 | O Lord of light, who made the stars |
| 328, 329 | All hail the pow'r of Jesus' name! |
| 363 | Christ is alive! Let Christians sing |
| 386 | Christ is the king! O friends, rejoice |
| 495 | Lead on, O King eternal |

## CHRIST THE KING (continued)

| | |
|---|---|
| **514** | O Savior, precious Savior |
| **530** | Jesus shall reign where'er the sun |
| **537** | O Jesus, king most wonderful |

## CHRISTMAS

*See 39-74*

| | |
|---|---|
| **30** | Come, thou long-expected Jesus |
| **75** | Bright and glorious is the sky |
| **86** | The only Son from Heaven |
| **180** | My soul now magnifies the Lord |
| **417** | In a lowly manger born |

## CHURCH

*See Community in Christ; Kingdom of God*

| | |
|---|---|
| **201** | O God of life's great mystery |
| **206** | Lord, who the night you were betrayed did pray |

## CHURCH BUILDING

*See Cornerstone*

| | |
|---|---|
| **367** | Christ is made the sure foundation |
| **375** | Only-begotten, Word of God eternal |

## CHURCH TRIUMPHANT

*See Hope*

| | |
|---|---|
| **27** | Lo! He comes with clouds descending |
| **182** | Rise, O children of salvation |
| **228, 229** | A mighty fortress is our God |
| **369** | The Church's one foundation |
| **377** | Lift high the cross, the love of Christ proclaim |
| **476** | Have no fear, little flock |

## CITY

*See Society*

| | |
|---|---|
| **418** | Judge eternal, throned in splendor |
| **419** | Lord of all nations, grant me grace |
| **427** | O Jesus Christ, may grateful hymns be rising |
| **429** | Where cross the crowded ways of life |
| **430** | Where restless crowds are thronging |
| **431** | Your hand, O Lord, in days of old |

CITY (continued)

| | |
|---|---|
| **434** | The Son of God, our Christ, the Word, the Way |
| **436** | All who love and serve your city |

**CLOSE OF SERVICE**

| | |
|---|---|
| | See 258-263 |
| **133** | Jesus lives! The vict'ry's won |
| **170** | Crown him with many crowns |
| **171** | Rejoice, the Lord is king! |
| **196** | Praise the Lord, rise up rejoicing |
| **219** | Come with us, O blessed Jesus |
| **221** | Sent forth by God's blessing |
| **227** | How blest are they who hear God's word |
| **230** | Lord, keep us steadfast in your Word |
| **231** | O Word of God incarnate |
| **234** | Almighty God, your Word is cast |
| **257** | Holy Spirit, truth divine |
| **259** | Lord, dismiss us with your blessing |
| **261** | On what has now been sown |
| **262** | Savior, again to your dear name we raise |
| **270** | God of our life, all-glorious Lord |
| **300** | O Christ, our hope, our hearts' desire |
| **316** | Jesus, the very thought of you |
| **320** | O God, our help in ages past |
| **328** | All hail the pow'r of Jesus' name |
| **335** | May God bestow on us his grace |
| **337** | Oh, what their joy and their glory must be |
| **338** | Peace, to soothe our bitter woes |
| **339** | O Lord, now let your servant |
| **343** | Guide me ever, great Redeemer |
| **345** | How sweet the name of Jesus sounds |
| **349** | I leave, as you have promised, Lord |
| **351** | Oh, happy day when we shall stand |
| **353** | May we your precepts, Lord, fulfill |
| **355** | Through the night of doubt and sorrow |
| **368** | I love your kingdom, Lord |
| **369** | The Church's one foundation |
| **370** | Blest be the tie that binds |
| **375** | Only-begotten, Word of God eternal |
| **376** | Your kingdom come! O Father, hear our prayer |
| **377** | Lift high the cross, the love of Christ proclaim |

## CLOSE OF SERVICE (continued)

| | |
|---|---|
| **379** | Spread, oh, spread, almighty Word |
| **381** | Hark, the voice of Jesus calling |
| **415** | God of grace and God of glory |
| **424** | Lord of glory, you have bought us |
| **425** | O God of mercy, God of might |
| **433** | The Church of Christ, in ev'ry age |
| **447** | All depends on our possessing |
| **460** | I am trusting you, Lord Jesus |
| **464** | You are the way; through you alone |
| **470** | Praise and thanks and adoration |
| **480** | Oh, that the Lord would guide my ways |
| **487** | Let us ever walk with Jesus |
| **495** | Lead on, O King eternal |
| **514** | O Savior, precious Savior |
| **518** | Beautiful Savior |
| **520** | Give to our God immortal praise! |
| **524** | My God, how wonderful thou art |
| **526** | Immortal, invisible, God only wise |
| **527** | All creatures of our God and King |
| **530** | Jesus shall reign where'er the sun |
| **533, 534** | Now thank we all our God |
| **535** | Holy God, we praise your name |
| **542** | Sing praise to God, the highest good |
| **545, 546** | When morning gilds the skies |
| **550** | From all that dwell below the skies |
| **551** | Joyful, joyful we adore thee |
| **553** | Rejoice, O pilgrim throng! |
| **559** | Oh, for a thousand tongues to sing |
| **564** | Praise God, from whom all blessings flow |

## COMFORT AND REST

| | |
|---|---|
| **106** | In the hour of trial |
| **272** | Abide with me, fast falls the eventide |
| **303** | When in the hour of deepest need |
| **319** | Oh, sing, my soul, your maker's praise |
| **338** | Peace, to soothe our bitter woes |
| **345** | How sweet the name of Jesus sounds |
| **346** | When peace, like a river, attendeth my way |
| **446** | Whatever God ordains is right |
| **450** | Who trusts in God, a strong abode |
| **451** | The Lord's my shepherd; I'll not want |
| **453** | If you but trust in God to guide you |
| **454** | If God himself be for me |

## COMFORT AND REST (continued)

| | |
|---|---|
| **456** | The King of love my shepherd is |
| **457,** | |
| **458** | Jesus, priceless treasure |
| **474** | Children of the heav'nly Father |
| **483** | God moves in a mysterious way |
| **493** | Hope of the world, thou Christ of great compassion |
| **504** | O God, my faithful God |

## COMMEMORATIONS AND OCCASIONS

Saints
| | |
|---|---|
| **176** | For all your saints, O Lord |

Martyrs
| | |
|---|---|
| **347** | Jerusalem the golden |
| **500** | Faith of our fathers, living still |

Missionaries
| | |
|---|---|
| **377** | Lift high the cross, the love of Christ proclaim |

Renewers of the Church
| | |
|---|---|
| **393** | Rise, shine, you people! Christ the Lord has entered |

Renewers of Society
| | |
|---|---|
| **363** | Christ is alive! Let Christians sing |

Pastors and Bishops
| | |
|---|---|
| **286** | Bow down your ear, almighty Lord |

Theologians
| | |
|---|---|
| **238** | God has spoken by his prophets |

Artists and Scientists
| | |
|---|---|
| **555** | When in our music God is glorified |
| | *See Creation* |

Unity
| | |
|---|---|
| | *See Unity* |
| **359** | In Christ there is no east or west |

Dedication, Anniversary
| | |
|---|---|
| **186** | How blessed is this place, O Lord |

Harvest
*See Harvest*

Day of Penitence
*See Repentance, Forgiveness; Sorrow*

National Holiday
*See National Songs; Society,*

Peace
*See Peace*

Day of Thanksgiving
*See Thanksgiving*

Stewardship of Creation
*See Creation; Harvest; Stewardship*

COMMEMORATIONS AND OCCASIONS (continued)

New Year's Eve
    See New Year

**COMMISSIONING, LAY MINISTRY**

    See Commitment

**COMMITMENT**

    See 486-513
| | |
|---|---|
| 106 | In the hour of trial |
| 243 | Lord, with glowing heart I'd praise thee |
| 305 | I lay my sins on Jesus |
| 323 | O Love that will not let me go |
| 336 | Jesus, thy boundless love to me |
| 339 | O Lord, now let your servant |
| 353 | May we your precepts, Lord, fulfill |
| 383 | Rise up, O saints of God! |
| 398 | "Take up your cross," the Savior said |
| 403 | Lord, speak to us, that we may speak |
| 406 | Take my life, that I may be |
| 444 | With the Lord begin your task |
| 461 | Fight the good fight with all your might |
| 474 | Children of the heav'nly Father |

**COMMUNION OF SAINTS**

    See Community in Christ

**COMMUNITY IN CHRIST**

    See 353-375
| | |
|---|---|
| 126 | Where charity and love prevail |
| 173 | The head that once was crowned with thorns |
| 228, 229 | A mighty fortress is our God |
| 255 | Lord, receive this company |
| 285 | Spirit of God, sent from heaven abroad |
| 307 | Forgive our sins as we forgive |
| 319 | Oh, sing, my soul, your maker's praise |
| 396 | O God, O Lord of heav'n and earth |
| 477 | O God of Jacob, by whose hand |
| 484 | God, my Lord, my strength, my place of hiding |
| 512 | Oh, blest the house, whate'er befall |
| 519 | My soul, now praise your maker! |

**CONFESSION OF SINS**

    *See Repentance, Forgiveness*

**CONFIRMATION**

    *See Affirmation of Baptism; Commitment; Pentecost*
| | |
|---|---|
| 192 | Baptized into your name most holy |
| 230 | Lord, keep us steadfast in your Word |

**CONSECRATION**

    *See Commitment*

**CORNERSTONE**

| | |
|---|---|
| 185 | Great God, a blessing from your throne |

    *See Church Building*

**COURAGE**

| | |
|---|---|
| 399 | We are the Lord's, His all-sufficient merit |

**CREATION**

| | |
|---|---|
| 242 | Let the whole creation cry |
| 362 | We plow the fields and scatter |
| 373 | Eternal Ruler of the ceaseless round |
| 391 | And have the bright immensities |
| 392 | O Lord, send forth your Spirit |
| 409 | Praise and thanksgiving |
| 411 | Lord of all good, our gifts we bring you now |
| 412 | Sing to the Lord of harvest |
| 415 | God of grace and God of glory |
| 416 | O God of every nation |
| 420 v3 | Lord, save your world in bitter need |
| 463 | God, who stretched the spangled heavens |
| 466 | Great God, our source and Lord of space |
| 515 | How marvelous God's greatness |
| 527 | All creatures of our God and King |
| 530 | Jesus shall reign where'er the sun |
| 541 | Praise the Lord of heaven |
| 548 | Oh, worship the King, all glorious above |
| 551 | Joyful, joyful we adore thee |
| 554 | This is my Father's world |
| 557 | Let all things now living |
| 558 v2 | Earth and all stars! |
| 560 | Oh, that I had a thousand voices |
| 561 | For the beauty of the earth |

**CREATION** (continued)

| | |
|---|---|
| **563** | For the fruit of all creation |

**CRISIS**

| | |
|---|---|
| **461** | Fight the good fight with all your might |

**CROSS-BEARING**

| | |
|---|---|
| **107** | Beneath the cross of Jesus |
| **115** | Jesus, I will ponder now |
| **398** | "Take up your cross," the Savior said |
| **455** | "Come, follow me," the Savior spake |
| **487** | Let us ever walk with Jesus |
| **504** | O God, my faithful God |
| | See Commitment |

**DEACONESSES AND DEACONS**

See Commitment; Pastors

**DEATH**

See Easter; Funeral

| | |
|---|---|
| **105** | A lamb goes uncomplaining forth |
| **116, 117** | O sacred head, now wounded |
| **133** | Jesus lives! The vict'ry's won! |
| **291** | Jesus sinners will recieve |
| **292** | God loved the world so that he gave |
| **339** | O Lord, now let your servant |
| **340** | Jesus Christ, my sure defense |
| **342** | I know of a sleep in Jesus' name |
| **343** | Guide me ever, great Redeemer |
| **350** | Even as we live each day |
| **399** | We are the Lords'. His all-sufficient merit |
| **435** | O God, whose will is life and good |
| **451** | The Lord's my shepherd; I'll not want |
| **456** | The King of love my shepherd is |
| **479** | My faith looks up to thee |
| **501** | He leadeth me: oh blessed thought |

**DEDICATION OF A CHURCH**

| | |
|---|---|
| **185** | Great God, a blessing from your throne |
| **186** | How blessed is this place, O Lord |
| **250** | Open now thy gates of beauty |
| **285** | Spirit of God, sent from heaven abroad |
| **358** | Glories of your name are spoken |

## DEDICATION OF A CHURCH (continued)

| | |
|---|---|
| 365 | Built on a rock the Church shall stand |
| 367 | Christ is made the sure foundation |
| 368 | I love your kingdom, Lord |
| 369 | The Church's one foundation |
| 375 | Only-begotten, Word of God eternal |
| 512 | Oh, blest the house whate'er befall |
| 533, 534 | How thank we all our God |

## DISCIPLESHIP

See Witness; Commitment

## EARTH

See Creation

## EASTER

See 128-155

| | |
|---|---|
| Cant. 13 | Keep in mind that Jesus Christ has died for us |
| 158 | Alleluia! Sing to Jesus |
| 175 | Ye watchers and ye holy ones |
| 189 | We know that Christ is raised and dies no more |
| 209 | Come, risen Lord, and deign to be our guest |
| 210 | At the Lamb's feast we sing |
| 258 | Hosanna to the Living Lord! |
| 300 | O Christ, our hope, our hearts' desire |
| 340 | Jesus Christ, my sure defense |
| 352 | I Know that my Redeemer lives! |
| 363 | Christ is alive! Let Christians sing |
| 391 | And have the bright immensities |

## EDUCATION

See Word

| | |
|---|---|
| 237 | O God of light, your Word, a lamp unfailing |
| 238 | God has spoken by his prophets |
| 239 | God's Word is our great heritage |
| 240 | Father of mercies, in your Word |
| 257 | Holy Spirit, truth divine |
| 367 | Christ is made the sure foundation |
| 403 | Lord, speak to us, that we may speak |
| 464 | You are the way; through you alone |

## EDUCATION (continued)

| | |
|---|---|
| **472, 473** | Come, Holy Ghost, our souls inspire |
| **495** | Lead on, O King eternal! |
| **510** | O God of youth, whose Spirit in our hearts is stirring |
| **558** | Earth and all stars! |

## ENTRANCE

*See Beginning of Service*

## EPIPHANY

*See 75-90*

| | |
|---|---|
| **50** | Angels, from the realms of glory |
| **56** | The first Noel the angel did say |
| **184** | In his temple now behold him |
| **198** | Let all mortal flesh keep silence |
| **205** | Now the silence |
| **232** | Your Word, O Lord, is gentle dew |
| **237** | O God of light, your Word, a lamp unfailing |
| **265** | Christ, whose glory fills the skies |
| **271** | O splendor of the Father's light |
| **273** | O Christ, you are the light and day |
| **300** | O Christ, our hope, our hearts' desire |
| **393** | Rise, shine, you people! Christ the Lord has entered |
| **400** | God, whose almighty word |
| **493** | Hope of the world, thou Christ of great compassion |
| **536** | O God of God, O Light of Light |
| **559** | Oh, for a thousand tongues to sing |
| **561** | For the beauty of the earth |

## ETERNAL LIFE

*See Hope; Life Everlasting*

## EVANGELISM

| | |
|---|---|
| **285** | Spirit of God, sent from heaven abroad |
| **425** | O God of mercy, God of light |
| **433** | The Church of Christ, in ev'ry age |
| **530** | Jesus shall reign where'er the sun |
| **556** | Herald, sound the note of judgement |
| **559** | Oh, for a thousand tongues to sing |

## EVANGELISM (continued)

See Witness

## EVENING

See 272-282

| | |
|---|---|
| 25 | Rejoice, rejoice, believers |
| 44 | Infant holy, infant lowly |
| 180 | My soul now magnifies the Lord |
| 262 | Savior, again to your dear name we raise |
| 263 | Abide with us, our Savior |
| 270 | God of our life, all-glorious Lord |
| 333 | Lord, take my hand and lead me |
| 334 | Jesus, Savior, pilot me |
| 339 | O Lord, now let your servant |
| 356 | O Jesus, joy of loving hearts |
| 444 | With the Lord begin your task |
| 465 | Evening and morning |
| 468 | From God can nothing move me |
| 470 | Praise and thanks and adoration |
| 542 | Sing praise to God, the highest good |
| 545, 546 | When morning gilds the skies |

## FAITH

| | |
|---|---|
| 327 | Rock of Ages, cleft for me |
| 340 | Jesus Christ, my sure defense |
| 356 | O Jesus, joy of loving hearts |
| 378 | Amid the world's bleak wilderness |
| 464 | You are the way; through you alone |
| 479 | My faith looks up to thee |
| 483 | God moves in a mysterious way |
| 492 | O Master, let me walk with you |
| 497 | I heard the voice of Jesus say |
| 500 | Faith of our fathers, living still |
| 507 | How firm a foundation, O saints of the Lord |

See Justification

## FAMILY

| | |
|---|---|
| 69 | I am so glad each Christmas Eve |
| 357 | Our Father, by whose name |
| 375 | Only-begotten, Word of God eternal |
| 474 | Children of the heav'nly Father |
| 512 | Oh, blest the house, whate'er befall |

**FAMILY** (continued)

    **561**    For the beauty of the earth

**FEAST OF JOHN THE BAPTIST**

    **29**    Comfort, comfort now my people

**FELLOWSHIP**

    See Community in Christ

**FORGIVENESS**

    See Repentance, Forgiveness

**FOURTH OF JULY**

| | |
|---|---|
| **414** | O God of love, O King of peace |
| **415** | God of grace and God of glory |
| **437** | Not alone for mighty empire |
| | See National Songs |

**FREEDOM**

| | |
|---|---|
| **p. 134** | The Gospel Canticle |
| **22** | The advent of our God |
| **26** | Prepare the royal highway |
| **30** | Come, thou long-expected Jesus |
| **246 v5** | The first day of the week |
| **257 v5** | Holy Spirit, truth divine |
| **393** | |
| **vv2, 4** | Rise, shine you people! Christ the Lord has entered |
| **396 v2** | O God, O Lord of heav'n and earth |
| **420** | Lord, save your world, in bitter need |
| **423 v2** | Lord, whose love in humble service |
| **433 v5** | The Church of Christ, in ev'ry age |
| **437 v2** | Not alone for mighty empire |
| **462 v4** | God the omnipotent! King who ordainest |
| **538 v4** | Oh, praise the Lord, my soul! |
| **544 v6** | The God of Abr'ham praise |
| **562 v1** | Lift ev'ry voice and sing |
| **566** | My country, 'tis of thee |
| **567** | God of our fathers, whose almighty hand |

**FRIEND**

    **457**    Jesus, priceless treasure

## FRIEND (continued)

| | |
|---|---|
| 485 | Lord, as a pilgrim through life I go |

## FUNERAL

*See Death; Easter*

| | |
|---|---|
| Cant. 13 | Keep in mind that Jesus Christ has died for us |
| 102 | On my heart imprint your image |
| 105 | A lamb goes uncomplaining forth |
| 129 | Awake, my heart, with gladness |
| 133 | Jesus lives! The vict'ry's won! |
| 135 | The strife is o'er, the battle done |
| 141 | The day of resurrection! |
| 174 | For all the saints who from their labors rest |
| 175 | Ye watchers and ye holy ones |
| 176 | For all your saints, O Lord |
| 219 | Come with us, O blessed Jesus |
| 263 | Abide with us, our Savior |
| 295 | Out of the depths I cry to you |
| 304 | Today your mercy calls us |
| 313 | A multitude comes from the east and the west |
| 314 | Who is this host arrayed in white |
| 315 | Love divine, all loves excelling |
| 317 | To God the Holy Spirit let us pray |
| 320 | O God, our help in ages past |
| 324 | O Love that will not let me go |
| 333 | Lord, take my hand and lead me |
| 334 | Jesus Savior, pilot me |
| 336 | Jesus, thy boundless love to me |
| 337 | Oh, what their joy and their glory must be |
| 338 | Peace, to soothe our bitter woes |
| 339 | O Lord, now let your servant |
| 340 | Jesus Christ, my sure defense |
| 341 | Jesus, still lead on |
| 342 | I know of a sleep in Jesus' name |
| 347 | Jerusalem the golden |
| 348 | Jerusalem, whose towers touch the sky |
| 350 | Even as we live each day |
| 351 | Oh, happy day when we shall stand |
| 352 | I know that my Redeemer lives |
| 399 | We are the Lord's. His all-sufficient merit |
| 445 | Unto the hills around do I lift up |
| 446 | Whatever God ordains is right |
| 447 | All depends on our possessing |
| 451 | The Lord's my shepherd, I'll not want |

**FUNERAL** (continued)

| | |
|---|---|
| 452 | As pants the hart for cooling streams |
| 453 | If you but trust in God to guide you |
| 456 | The King of love my shepherd is |
| 459 | O Holy Spirit, enter in |
| 474 | Children of the heav'nly Father |
| 479 | My faith looks up to thee |
| 489 | Wide open are your hands |
| 532 | How great Thou art |

**GOOD FRIDAY**

*See Holy Week*

| | |
|---|---|
| 92 | Were you there when they crucified my Lord |
| 101 | O Christ, our king, creator, Lord |
| 107 | Beneath the cross of Jesus |
| 168 | Kyrie! God, Father in heaven above |
| 479 | My faith looks up to thee |
| 482 | When I survey the wondrous cross |
| 489 | Wide open are your hands |

**GOD'S HAND**

| | |
|---|---|
| 333 | Lord, take my hand and lead me |
| 343 | Guide me ever, great Redeemer |
| 424 | Lord of glory, you have bought us |
| 431 | Your hand, O Lord, in days of old |
| 477 | O God of Jacob, by whose hand |
| 489 | Wide open are your hands |
| 501 | He leadeth me: oh, blessed thought |

**GRACE**

| | |
|---|---|
| 98 | Alas! And did my Savior bleed |
| 290 | There's a wideness in God's mercy |
| 315 | Love divine, all loves excelling |
| 356 | O Jesus, joy of loving hearts |
| 488 | Amazing grace, how sweet the sound |
| 489 | Wide open are your hands |
| 499 | Come, thou Fount of ev'ry blessing |
| 520 | Give to our God immortal praise! |
| 549 | Praise, my soul, the King of heaven |

**GUIDANCE**

*See Trust, Guidance*

## HARVEST

| | |
|---|---|
| 362 | We plow the fields and scatter |
| 404 | As saints of old their first fruits brought |
| 407 | Come, you thankful people, come |
| 409 | Praise and thanksgiving |
| 412 | Sing to the Lord of harvest |
| 533, 534 | Now thank we all our God |

See Creation

## HEALING

| | |
|---|---|
| 36 | On Jordan's banks the Baptist's cry |
| 194 | All who believe and are baptized |
| 292 | God loved the world so that he gave |
| 341 | Jesus, still lead on |
| 360 | O Christ, the healer, we have come |
| 400 | God, whose almighty word |
| 418 | Judge, eternal, throned in splendor |
| 422 | O God, empower us to stem |
| 423 | Lord, whose love in humble service |
| 426 | O Son of God, in Galilee |
| 431 | Your hand, O Lord, in days of old |
| 435 | O God, whose will is life and good |
| 439 | What a friend we have in Jesus |
| 485 | Lord, as a pilgrim through life I go |
| 544 | The God of Abraham praise |

## HEAVEN

| | |
|---|---|
| 73 | All hail to you, O blessed morn! |
| 313 | A multitude comes from the east and the west |
| 314 | Who is this host arrayed in white |
| 330 | In Heav'n above, in heav'n above |
| 331 | Jerusalem, my happy home |
| 337 | Oh, what their joy and their glory must be |
| 348 | Jerusalem whose towers touch the skies |
| 351 | Oh, happy day when we shall stand |
| 560 | Oh, that I had a thousand voices |

## HOLINESS

See Justification; Pentecost; Trust, Guidance

## HOLY BAPTISM

See 187-195
See Commitment; Trust
- **79** To Jordan came the Christ, our Lord
- **282** Now rest beneath night's shadow
- **292** God loved the world so that he gave
- **350** Even as we live each day
- **375** Only-begotten, Word of God eternal

## HOLY COMMUNION

See 196-226
- **24** Come, O precious Ransom, come
- **78** All praise to you, O Lord
- **120** Of the glorious body telling
- **127** It happened on that fateful night
- **158** Alleluia! Sing to Jesus
- **172** Lord, enthroned in heav'nly splendor
- **227** How blest are they who hear God's word
- **235** Break now the bread of life
- **255** Lord, receive this company
- **291** Jesus sinners will receive
- **292** God loved the world so that he gave
- **296** Just as I am, without one plea
- **301** Come to Calv'ry's holy mountain
- **302** Jesus, your blood and righteousness
- **305** I lay my sins on Jesus
- **316** Jesus, the very thought of you
- **325** Lord, thee I love with all my heart
- **327** Rock of Ages, cleft for me
- **345** How sweet the name of Jesus sounds
- **356** O Jesus, joy of loving hearts
- **371** With God as our friend, with his Spirit and Word
- **375** Only-begotten, Word of God eternal
- **391** And have the bright immensities
- **448** Amazing grace, how sweet the sound
- **452** As pants the hart for cooling streams
- **456** The King of love my shepherd is
- **457** Jesus, priceless treasure
- **460** I am trusting you Lord Jesus
- **479** My faith looks up to thee
- **482** When I survey the wondrous cross
- **496** Around you, O Lord Jesus
- **511** Renew me, O eternal Light
- **513** Come, my way, my truth, my life
- **516** Arise, my soul, arise!
- **528** Isaiah in a vision did of old

See Praise, Adoration

## HOLY CROSS DAY

| 118 | Sing, my tongue, the glorious battle |
| 344 | We sing the praise of him who died |
| 482 | When I survey the wondrous cross |

## HOLY INNOCENTS, MARTYRS

| 177, 178 | By all your saints in warfare |

## HOLY LAND

| 41 | O little town of Bethlehem |
| 81 | O chief of cities, Bethlehem |
| 449 | They cast their nets in Galilee |
| 494 | Jesus calls us; o'er the tumult |
| 506 | Dear Lord and Father of mankind |

## HOLY SATURDAY

| 92 | Were you there when they crucified my Lord |
| 109 | Go to dark Gethsemane |
| 146 | Rejoice, angelic choirs, rejoice |
| 173 | The head that once was crowned with thorns |
| 188 | I bind unto myself today |
| 350 | Even as we live each day |

## HOLY SPIRIT

See Commitment; Pentecost; Trust, Guidance; Witness

| 189 | We know that Christ is raised |
| 257 | Holy Spirit, truth divine |
| 284 | Creator Spirit, heav'nly dove |
| 317 | To God the Holy Spirit let us pray |
| 472, 473 | Come, Holy Ghost, our souls inspire |
| 475 | Come, gracious Spirit, heav'nly dove |
| 478 | Come, oh, come, O quick'ning Spirit |
| 488 | Breathe on me, breath of God |
| 508 | Come down, O love divine |
| 511 | Renew me, O eternal Light |

## HOLY TRINITY

See 165-169

## HOLY TRINITY (continued)

| | |
|---|---|
| 188 | I bind unto myself today |
| 191 | Praise and thanksgiving be to God |
| 230 | Lord, keep us steadfast in your Word |
| 238 | God has spoken by his prophets |
| 242 | Let the whole creation cry |
| 247 | Holy Majesty, before you |
| 248 | Dearest Jesus, at your word |
| 257 | Holy Spirit, truth divine |
| 266 | Maker of the earth and heaven |
| 267 | Father, we praise you, now the night is over |
| 275 | O Trinity, O blessed Light |
| 284 | Creator Spirit, heav'nly dove |
| 308 | God the Father, be our stay |
| 353 | May we your precepts, Lord, fulfill |
| 354 | Eternal God, before your throne we bend |
| 357 | Our Father, by whose name |
| 373 | Eternal Ruler of the ceaseless round |
| 374 | We all believe in one true God |
| 393 | Rise, shine, you people! |
| 396 | O God, O Lord of heav'n and earth |
| 400 | God, whose almighty word |
| 425 | O God of mercy, God of light |
| 467 | Eternal Father, strong to save |
| 472, 473 | Come, Holy Ghost, our souls inspire |
| 490 | Let me be yours forever |
| 517 | Praise to the Father |
| 522 | Come, thou almighty King |
| 535 | Holy God, we praise your name |
| 544 | The God of Abr'ham praise |

## HOLY WEEK

*See 108-127*

| | |
|---|---|
| 489 | Wide open are your hands |

## HOME

*See Family*

## HOPE (CHRISTIAN HOPE)

*See 313-352*

| | |
|---|---|
| 33 | The King shall come when morning dawns |

## HOPE (CHRISTIAN HOPE) (continued)

| | |
|---|---|
| 38 | O Savior, rend the heavens wide |
| 133 | Jesus lives! The vict'ry's won! |
| 161 | O day full of grace that now we see |
| 168 | Kyrie! God, Father in heav'n above |
| 182 | Rise, O children of salvation |
| 244 | Lord our God, with praise we come before you |
| 326 | My heart is longing to praise my Savior |
| 358 | Glories of your name are spoken |
| 384 | Your kingdom come, O Father |
| 387 | Spirit of God, unleashed on earth |
| 426 | O Son of God, in Galilee |
| 432 | We worship you, O God of might |
| 452 | As pants the hart for cooling streams |
| 453 | If you but trust in God to guide you |
| 487 | Let us ever walk with Jesus |
| 493 | Hope of the world, thou Christ of great compassion |

See Heaven; Life Everlasting

## HOSPITALS

See Healing

## HOUSE OF GOD

See Church Building; Dedication of a Church

## HUMILITY

| | |
|---|---|
| 309 | Lord Jesus, think on me |
| 310 | To you, omniscient Lord of all |
| 438 | Lord, teach us how to pray aright |
| 508 | Come down, O Love divine |

## IMMORTALITY

See Hope; Life Everlasting

## INCARNATION

| | |
|---|---|
| 198 | Let all mortal flesh keep silence |

## INNER LIFE

| | |
|---|---|
| 211 | Here, O my Lord, I see thee face to face |
| 316 | Jesus, the very thought of you |

**INNER LIFE** (continued)

| | |
|---|---|
| 336 | Jesus, thy boundless love to me |
| 345 | How sweet the name of Jesus sounds |
| 441 | Eternal Spirit of the living Christ |
| 488 | Breathe on me, breath of God |
| 486 | Spirit of God, descend upon my heart |
| 501 | He leadeth me: oh, blessed thought! |
| 506 | Dear Lord and Father of mankind |
| 508 | Come Down, O Love divine |
| 537 | O Jesus, king most wonderful |

**INSTALLATION**

See Pastors

**INVITATION**

| | |
|---|---|
| 290 | There's a wideness in God's mercy |
| 291 | Jesus sinners will receive |
| 301 | Come to Calv'ry's holy mountain |
| 304 | Today your mercy calls us |
| 381 | Hark, the voice of Jesus calling |
| 494 | Jesus calls us; o'er the tumult |
| 497 | I heard the voice of Jesus say |

**INVOCATION**

| | |
|---|---|
| 275 | O Trinity, O blessed Light |
| 354 | Eternal God, before your throne we bend |
| 459 | O Holy Spirit, enter in |
| 472, 473 | Come, Holy Ghost, our souls inspire |
| 508 | Come down, O Love divine |
| 522 | Come, thou almighty King |
| 535 | Holy God, we praise your name |

See Beginning of Service

**JERUSALEM**

| | |
|---|---|
| 331 | Jerusalem, my happy home |
| 347 | Jerusalem the golden |
| 348 | Jerusalem, whose towers touch the skies |

**JUDGMENT**

| | |
|---|---|
| 27 | Lo! He comes with clouds descending |

## JUDGMENT (continued)

| | |
|---|---|
| 31 | Wake, awake, for night is flying |
| 33 | The King shall come when morning dawns |
| 318 | The Lord will come and not be slow |
| 321 | The day is surely drawing near |
| 322 | The clouds of judgment gather |
| 323 | O Lord of light, who made the stars |
| 332 | Battle Hymn of the Republic |
| 388 | O Spirit of the living God |
| 418 | Judge eternal, throned in splendor |
| 556 | Herald, sound the note of judgment |

## JUSTIFICATION

*See 290-301*

| | |
|---|---|
| 173 | The head that once was crowned with thorns |
| 326 | My heart is longing to praise my Savior |
| 346 | When peace, like a river, attendeth my way |
| 374 | We all believe in one true God |
| 385 | What wondrous love is this, O my soul, O my soul! |
| 424 | Lord of glory, you have brought us |
| 454 | If God himself be for me |
| 489 | Wide open are your hands |
| 490 | Let me be yours forever |
| 491 | O God, I love thee; not that my poor love |
| 519 | My soul, now praise your maker! |

## KINGDOM OF GOD

| | |
|---|---|
| 87 | Hail to the Lord's anointed |
| 230 | Lord, keep us steadfast in your Word |
| 318 | The Lord will come and not be slow |
| 368 | I love your kingdom, Lord |
| 376 | Your kingdom come! O Father, hear our prayer |
| 384 | Your kingdom come, O Father |
| 413 | Father eternal, ruler of creation |

*See Community in Christ*

## LABOR, LABORERS, LABOR DAY

*See Society; Work, Daily*

| | |
|---|---|
| 469 | Lord of all hopefulness, Lord of all joy |

## LABOR, LABORERS, LABOR DAY (continued)

| | |
|---|---|
| **505** | Forth in thy name, O Lord, I go |

## LAST THINGS

See Hope; Judgment

## LENT

See 91-107

| | |
|---|---|
| **27** | Lo! He comes with clouds descending |
| **37** | Hark! A thrilling voice is sounding |
| **88** | Oh, love, how deep, how broad, how high |
| **115** | Jesus, I will ponder now |
| **182** | Rise, O children of salvation |
| **202** | Victim Divine, your grace we claim |
| **291** | Jesus sinners will receive |
| **292** | God loved the world so that he gave |
| **301** | Come to Calv'ry's holy mountain |
| **302** | Jesus, your blood and righteousness |
| **303** | When in the hour of deepest need |
| **308** | God the Father, be our stay |
| **325** | Lord, thee I love with all my heart |
| **326** | My heart is longing to praise my Savior |
| **344** | We sing the praise of him who died |
| **367** | Christ is made the sure foundation |
| **372** | In Adam we have all been one |
| **385** | What wondrous love is this, O my soul, O my soul |
| **395** | I trust, O Christ, in you alone |
| **420** | Lord, save your world; in bitter need |
| **421** | Lord Christ, when first you come to earth |
| **424** | Lord of glory, you have brought us |
| **443** | Rise, my soul, to watch and pray |
| **479** | My faith looks up to thee |
| **482** | When I survey the wondrous cross |
| **489** | Wide open are your hands |
| **491** | O God, I love thee; not that my poor love |

## LESSER FESTIVALS

See 174-186

## LIFE, CHRISTIAN

| | |
|---|---|
| **102** | On my heart imprint your image |

## LIFE, CHRISTIAN (continued)

| | |
|---|---|
| 315 | Love divine, all loves excelling |
| 425 | O God of mercy, God of light |
| 480 | Oh, that the Lord would guide my ways |
| 487 | Let us ever walk with Jesus |
| 492 | O Master, let me walk with you |
| 503 | O Jesus, I have promised |
| 504 | O God, my faithful God |

See Commitment; Justification; Trust, Guidance

## LIFE EVERLASTING

| | |
|---|---|
| 76 | O Morning Star, how fair and bright! |
| 337 | Oh, what their joy and their glory must be |
| 385 | What wondrous love is this, O my soul, O my soul! |
| 490 | Let me be yours forever |
| 516 | Arise, my soul, arise! |
| 544 | The God of Abr'ham praise |

See Hope, Christian

## LORD'S PRAYER

| | |
|---|---|
| 376 | Your kingdom come |
| 442 | O thou, who hast of thy pure grace |

## LORD'S SUPPER

See Holy Communion

## LOVE

| | |
|---|---|
| 93 | Jesus, refuge of the weary |
| 298 | One there is, above all others |
| 306 | Chief of sinners though I be |
| 336 | Jesus, thy boundless love to me |
| 359 | In Christ there is no east or west |
| 364 | Son of God, eternal Savior |
| 370 | Blest be the tie that binds |
| 385 | What wondrous love is this, O my soul, O my soul! |
| 403 | Lord, speak to us, that we may speak |
| 414 | O God of love, O King of peace |
| 419 | Lord of all nations, grant me grace |
| 429 | Where cross the crowded ways of life |

## LOVE (continued)

| | |
|---|---|
| **491** | O God, I love thee; not that my poor love |
| **492** | O Master, let me walk with you |
| **502** | Thee will I love, my strength, my tow'r |
| **551** | Joyful, joyful we adore thee |

## MARRIAGE

See Wedding
See 287-289

## MARTYRS

See Commemorations and Occasions

## MARY, MOTHER OF OUR LORD

See Saints' Days

## MAUNDY THURSDAY

See Holy Week

| | |
|---|---|
| **199** | Thee we adore, O hidden Savior |
| **206** | Lord, the night you were betrayed did pray |
| **207** | We who once were dead |
| **209** | Come, risen Lord, and deign to be our guest |
| **214** | Come, let us eat, for now the feast is spread |
| **215** | O Lord, we praise you, bless you, and adore you |

## MEANS OF GRACE

See Holy Baptism; Holy Communion; The Word

## MEETINGS

| | |
|---|---|
| **444** | With the Lord begin your task |

## MERCY

| | |
|---|---|
| **264** | When all your mercies, O my God |
| **290** | There's a wideness in God's mercy |
| **295** | Out of the depths I cry to you |

MERCY (continued)

| | |
|---|---|
| 315 | Love divine, all loves excellling |
| 417 | In a lowly manger born |
| 425 | O God of mercy, God of light |
| 521 | Let us with a gladsome mind |

**MISSION, MISSIONS**

See Commitment; Pilgrimage; Society; Witness

| | |
|---|---|
| 122 | Love consecrates the humblest act |
| 237 | O God of light, your Word, a lamp unfailing |
| 531 | Before Jehovah's awesome throne |
| 550 | From all that dwell below the skies |

**MORNING**

See 262-271

| | |
|---|---|
| 371 | With God as our friend, with his Spirit and Word |
| 444 | With the Lord begin your task |
| 465 | Evening and morning |
| 468 | From God can nothing move me |
| 469 | Lord of all hopefulness, Lord of all joy |
| 470 | Praise and thanks and adoration |
| 542 | Sing praise to God, the highest good |
| 545, 546 | When morning gilds the skies |

**MUSIC**

See Arts and Music

**NAME OF JESUS, THE**

| | |
|---|---|
| 179 | At the name of Jesus |
| 328, 329 | All hail the pow'r of Jesus' name |
| 345 | How sweet the name of Jesus sounds |
| 514 | O Savior, precious Savior |
| 559 | Oh, for a thousand tongues to sing |

**NATIONAL SONGS**

| | |
|---|---|
| 332 | Battle Hymn of the Republic |
| 401 | Before you, Lord, we bow |
| 416 | O God of ev'ry nation |
| 418 | Judge eternal, throned in splendor |
| 428 | O God of earth and altar |

## NATIONAL SONGS (continued)

| | |
|---|---|
| 437 | Not alone for mighty empire |
| 462 | God the omnipotent! King who ordainest |
| 466 | Great God our source and Lord of space |
| 467 | Eternal Father, strong to save |
| 538 | Oh, praise the Lord, my soul! |
| 562 | Lift ev'ry voice and sing |
| 566 | My country, 'tis of thee |
| 567 | God of our Fathers |
| 568 | God save our gracious queen |
| 569 | God bless our native land |
| | See Society |

## NATURE

| | |
|---|---|
| 119 | Nature with open volume stands |
| 409 | Praise and thanksgiving |
| 527 | All creatures of our God and King |
| 551 | Joyful, joyful we adore thee |
| 557 | Let all things now living |
| 560 | Oh, that I had a thousand voices |
| 561 | For the beauty of the earth |
| | See Creation |

## NEIGHBOR

See Commitment; Love; Society; Service

## NEW YEAR

| | |
|---|---|
| 179 | At the name of Jesus |
| 181 | Greet now the swiftly changing year |
| 320 | O God, our help in ages past |
| 345 | How sweet the name of Jesus sounds |
| 447 | All depends on our possessing |
| 465 | Evening and morning |
| 477 | O God of Jacob, by whose hand |
| 480 | Oh, that the Lord would guide my ways |
| 485 | Lord, as a pilgrim through life I go |
| 497 | I heard the voice of Jesus say |
| 533, 534 | Now thank we all our God |

## OBEDIENCE

See Service

**OCCASIONS**

See Commemorations and Occasions

**OFFERINGS**

See Stewardship

**OFFERTORY**

| | |
|---|---|
| 217 | We place upon your table, Lord |
| 255 | Lord, receive this company |
| 404 | As saints of old their first fruits brought |
| 406 | Take my life, that I may be |
| 410 | We give thee but thine own |
| 411 | Lord of all good, our gifts we bring you now |

**ORDINATION**

See Pastors; Pentecost

**PALM SUNDAY (SUNDAY OF THE PASSION)**

See Holy Week

| | |
|---|---|
| 23 | O Lord, how shall I meet you |
| 26 | Prepare the royal highway |
| 35 | Hark, the glad sound! The Savior comes |
| 74 | A stable lamp is lighted |
| 183 | The Son of God goes forth to war |
| 258 | Hosanna to the living Lord! |
| 375 | Only-begotten, Word of God eternal |

**PARENTS**

| | |
|---|---|
| 440 | Christians, while on earth abiding |

**PASSION OF CHRIST**

See Holy Week

**PASSION, SUNDAY OF THE**

See Holy Week; Palm Sunday

**PASTORS**

See 283-286

| | |
|---|---|
| 164 | Creator Spirit, by whose aid |

## PASTORS (continued)

| | |
|---|---|
| 387 | Spirit of God, unleashed on earth |
| 472, 473 | Come, Holy Ghost, our souls inspire |
| 478 | Come, oh, come, O quick'ning Spirit |
| 523 | Holy Spirit, ever dwelling |

## PEACE

| | |
|---|---|
| 262 | Savior, again to your name we raise |
| 338 | Peace, to soothe our bitter woes |
| 339 | O Lord, now let your servant |
| 363 | Christ is alive! Let Christians sing |
| 364 | Son of God, eternal Savior |
| 366 | Lord of our life and God of our salvation |
| 413 | Father eternal, ruler of creation |
| 414 | O God of love, O King of peace |
| 415 | God of grace and God of glory |
| 416 | O God of ev'ry nation |
| 421 | Lord Christ, when first you came to earth |
| 422 | O God empower us to stem |
| 437 | Not alone for mighty empire |
| 462 | God the omnipotent! King who ordainest |
| 466 | Great God, our source and Lord of space |
| 471 | Grant peace, we pray, in mercy, Lord |

## PENITENCE

See Repentance, Forgiveness

## PENTECOST

See 160-164

| | |
|---|---|
| 142 | Hail thee, festival day! |
| 257 | Holy Spirit, truth divine |
| 284 | Creator Spirit, heav'nly dove |
| 285 | Spirit of God, sent from heaven abroad |
| 317 | To God the Holy Spirit let us pray |
| 387 | Spirit of God, unleashed on earth |
| 388 | O Spirit of the living God |
| 392 | O Lord, send forth your Spirit |
| 441 | Eternal Spirit of the living Christ |
| 459 | O Holy Spirit, enter in |
| 472, 473 | Come, Holy Ghost, our souls inspire |

## PENTECOST (continued)

| | |
|---|---|
| **475** | Come, gracious Spirit, heav'nly dove |
| **478** | Come, oh, come, O quick'ning Spirit |
| **486** | Spirit of God, descend upon my heart |
| **488** | Breathe on me, breath of God |
| **508** | Come down, O Love divine |
| **511** | Renew me, O eternal Light |
| **523** | Holy Spirit, ever dwelling |
| | *See Trust, Guidance; Witness; Commitment* |

## PILGRIMAGE

| | |
|---|---|
| **83** | From God the Father, virgin-born |
| **108** | All glory, laud and honor |
| **222** | O Bread of life from heaven |
| **227** | How blest are they who hear God's Word |
| **231** | O Word of God incarnate |
| **259** | Lord, dismiss us with your blessing |
| **270** | God of our life, all-glorious Lord |
| **275** | O Trinity, O blessed Light |
| **334** | Jesus, Savior, pilot me |
| **340** | Jesus Christ, my sure defense |
| **341** | Jesus, still lead on |
| **343** | Guide me ever, great Redeemer |
| **355** | Through the night of doubt and sorrow |
| **451** | The Lord's my shepherd, I'll not want |
| **456** | The King of love my shepherd is |
| **467** | Eternal Father, strong to save |
| **475** | Come, gracious Spirit, heav'nly dove |
| **476** | Have no fear, little flock |
| **477** | O God of Jacob, by whose hand |
| **480** | Oh, that the Lord would guide my ways |
| **481** | Savior, like a shepherd lead us |
| **485** | Lord, as a pilgrim through life I go |
| **487** | Let us ever walk with Jesus |
| **497** | I heard the voice of Jesus say |
| **498** | All who would valiant be |
| **501** | He leadeth me: oh, blessed thought! |

## PLAINSONGS

| | |
|---|---|
| **34** | Oh, come, oh, come, Emmanuel |
| **42** | Of the Fathr's love begotten |
| **49** | O Savior of our fallen race |
| **64** | From east to west |

| | |
|---|---|
| 120 | Of the glorious body telling |
| 125 | The royal banners forward go |
| 137 | Christians, to the paschal victim |
| 168 | Kyrie, God Father in heav'n above |
| 199 | Thee we adore, O hidden Savior |
| 271 | O splendor of the Father's light |
| 277 | To you, before the close of day |
| 323 | O Lord of light, who made the stars |
| 441 | Eternal Spirit of the living Christ |
| 471 | Grant peace, we pray, in mercy Lord |
| 472 | Come, Holy Ghost, our souls inspire |

**PRAISE, ADORATION**

| | |
|---|---|
| | *See 514-551* |
| 166 | All glory be to God on high |
| 167 | Glory be to God the Father |
| 171 | Rejoice, the Lord is King! |
| 180 | My soul now magnifies the Lord |
| 191 | Praise and thanksgiving be to God our Maker |
| 233 | Thy strong word did cleave the darkness |
| 241 | We praise you, O God, our redeemer, creator |
| 242 | Let the whole creation cry |
| 243 | Lord, with glowing heart I'd praise thee |
| 244 | Lord our God, with praise we come before you |
| 245 | All people that on earth do dwell |
| 247 | Holy Majesty, before you |
| 249 | God himself is present |
| 252 | You servants of God, your master proclaim |
| 254 | Come, let us join our cheerful songs |
| 256 | Oh, sing jubilee to the Lord, ev'ry land |
| 258 | Hosanna to the living Lord! |
| 259 | Lord, dismiss us with your blessing |
| 264 | When all your mercies, O my God |
| 275 | O Trinity, O blessed Light |
| 326 | My heart is longing to praise my Savior |
| 328, 329 | All hail the pow'r of Jesus' name |
| 344 | We sing the praise of him who died |
| 345 | How sweet the name of Jesus sounds |
| 377 | Lift high the cross, the love of Christ proclaim |
| 409 | Praise and thanksgiving |
| 470 | Praise and thanks and adoration |
| 523 | Holy Spirit, ever dwelling |

**PRAYER**

    *See 438-444*
  **230**  Lord, keep us steadfast in your Word
  **371**  With God as our friend, with his Spirit and Word

**PRESENTATION OF OUR LORD, THE**

  **79**  To Jordan came the Christ, our Lord
  **184**  In his temple now behold him

**PROCESSIONS**

  **142**  Hail thee, festival day!
  **377**  Lift high the cross, the love of Christ proclaim
  **553**  Rejoice, O pilgrim throng!
    *See Beginning of Service*

**PROCLAMATION**

    *See Word; Witness*

**PROVIDENCE**

    *See Creation; Thanksgiving Day*

**RACES AND CULTURES**

  **221**  Sent forth by God's blessing
  **359**  In Christ there is no east or west
    *See Community in Christ; Society*

**RECEPTION**

    *See Affirmation of Baptism; Community in Christ*

**REDEEMER**

  **231**  O Word of God incarnate
  **248**  Dearest Jesus, at your word
  **253**  Lord Jesus Christ, be present now
  **258**  Hosanna to the living Lord
  **262**  Savior, again to your dear name we raise
  **263**  Abide with us, our Savior
  **265**  Christ whose glory fills the skies
  **273**  O Christ, you are the light and day

## REDEEMER (continued)

| | |
|---|---|
| 291 | Jesus sinners will receive |
| 292 | God loved the world so that he gave |
| 294 | My hope is built on nothing less |
| 300 | O Christ, our hope, our hearts' desire |
| 302 | Jesus, your blood and righteousness |
| 305 | I lay my sins on Jesus |
| 309 | Lord Jesus think on me |
| 315 | Love divine, all loves excelling |
| 316 | Jesus, the very thought of you |
| 327 | Rock of Ages, cleft for me |
| 328 | All hail the pow'r of Jesus' name |
| 334 | Jesus, Savior, pilot me |
| 336 | Jesus, thy boundless love to me |
| 340 | Jesus Christ, my sure defense |
| 341 | Jesus, still lead on |
| 345 | How sweet the name of Jesus sounds |
| 352 | I know that my Redeemer lives |
| 356 | O Jesus, joy of loving hearts |
| 363 | Christ is alive! Let Christians sing |
| 364 | Son of God, eternal Savior |
| 367 | Christ is made the sure foundation |
| 380 | O Christ, our light, O Radiance true |
| 381 | Hark, the voice of Jesus calling |
| 389 | Stand up, stand up for Jesus |
| 390 | I love to tell the story |
| 395 | I trust, O Christ, in you alone |
| 398 | "Take up your cross", the Savior said |
| 417 | In a lowly manger born |
| 421 | Lord Christ, when first you came to earth |
| 424 | Lord of glory, you have bought us |
| 427 | O Jesus Christ, may grateful hymns be rising |
| 434 | The Son of God, our Christ, the Word, the Way |
| 439 | What a friend we have in Jesus |
| 444 | With the Lord begin your task |
| 451 | The Lord's my shepherd; I'll not want |
| 455 | "Come, follow me," the Savior spake |
| 456 | The King of love my shepherd is |
| 457 | Jesus, priceless treasure |
| 460 | I am trusting you, Lord Jesus |
| 461 | Fight the good fight with all your might |
| 464 | You are the way; through you alone |
| 479 | My faith looks up to thee |
| 481 | Savior, like a shepherd lead us |

REDEEMER (continued)

| | |
|---|---|
| 484 | God, my Lord, my strength, my place of hiding |
| 487 | Let us ever walk with Jesus |
| 489 | Wide open are your hands |
| 491 | O God, I love thee; not that my poor love |
| 492 | O Master, let me walk with you |
| 493 | Hope of the world, thou Christ of great compassion |
| 494 | Jesus calls us; o'er the tumult |
| 496 | Around you, O Lord Jesus |
| 497 | I heard the voice of Jesus say |
| 503 | O Jesus, I have promised |
| 514 | O Savior, precious Savior |
| 518 | Beautiful Savior |
| 530 | Jesus shall reign where'er the sun |
| 536 | O God of God, O Light of Light |
| 537 | O Jesus, king most wonderful |
| 545, 546 | When morning gilds the skies |
| 552 | In thee is gladness |
| 558 | Earth and all stars |
| 559 | Oh, for a thousand tongues to sing |
| 561 | For the beauty of the earth |

See Christ the King; Holy Communion; Justification

## REFORMATION

| | |
|---|---|
| 228, 229 | A mighty fortress is our God |
| 230 | Lord, keep us steadfast in your Word |
| 239 | God's Word is our great heritage |
| 297 | Salvation unto us has come |
| 299 | Dear Christians, one and all, rejoice |
| 361 | Do not despair, O little flock |
| 365 | Built on a rock the Church shall stand |
| 369 | The Church's one foundation |
| 372 | In Adam we have all been one |
| 395 | I trust, O Christ, in you alone |
| 396 | O God, O Lord of heav'n and earth |
| 500 | Faith of our fathers, living still |

See Community in Christ; Justification

## REPENTANCE, FORGIVENESS

See 303-312

## REPENTANCE, FORGIVENESS (continued)

| | |
|---|---|
| 91 | Savior, when in dust to you |
| 98 | Alas! And did my Savior bleed |
| 211 | Here, O my Lord, I see thee face to face |
| 215 | O Lord, we praise you |
| 295 | Out of the depths I cry to you |
| 297 | Salvation unto us has come |
| 301 | Come to Calv'ry's holy mountain |
| 304 | Today your mercy calls us |
| 395 | I trust, O Christ, in you alone |
| 419 | Lord of all nations, grant me grace |
| 440 | Christians, while on earth abiding |
| 443 | Rise, my soul, to watch and pray |
| 448 | Amazing grace, how sweet the sound |
| 450 | Who trusts in God, a strong abode |

## REST

See Comfort and Rest

## RESTORATION

See Affirmation of Baptism; Commitment; Repentance, Forgiveness

## RESURRECTION

See Easter; Hope, Christian

## ROGATION

See Creation; Thanksgiving, Day of

## SAINTS' DAYS

| | |
|---|---|
| 176 | For all your saints, O Lord |
| 177, 178 | By all your saints in warfare |
| 182 | Rise, O children of salvation |

St. Andrew, Apostle
| | |
|---|---|
| 494 | Jesus calls us; o'er the tumult |

St. Thomas
| | |
|---|---|
| 139 | O sons and daughters of the King |
| 325 | Lord, thee I love with all my heart |
| 464 | You are the way; through you alone |

St. Stephen, Deacon and Martyr
| | |
|---|---|
| 183 | The Son of God goes forth to war |

## SAINTS' DAYS (continued)

Confession of Saint Peter
- **491**    O God, I love thee, not that my poor love

Conversion of St. Paul
- **392**    O Lord, send forth your Spirit

St. Peter and St. Paul, Apostles
- **173**    The head that once was crowned with thorns

St. Mary Magdalene
- **147**    Hallelujah! Jesus lives!

Mary, Mother of Our Lord
- **110**    At the cross, her station keeping
- **175**    Ye watchers and ye holy ones
- **180**    My soul now magnifies the Lord

St. Michael and All Angels
- **249**    God himself is present

## SALVATION

*See Grace; Justification*

## SANCTIFICATION

*See Commitment; Pentecost; Trust, Guidance*

## SCHOOLS

*See Education*

## SCRIPTURES

- **227**    How blest are they who hear God's Word
- **237**    O God of light, your Word a lamp unfailing
- **240**    Father of mercies, in your Word

*See Word*

## SECOND COMING OF CHRIST

*See Hope; Judgment; Watchfulness*

## SERVICE

- **122**    Love consecrates the humblest act
- **160**    Filled with the Spirit's pow'r, with one accord

## SERVICE (continued)

| | |
|---|---|
| **359** | In Christ there is no east or west |
| **364** | Son of God, eternal Savior |
| **404** | As saints of old their first fruits brought |
| **408** | God, whose giving knows no ending |
| **410** | We give thee but thine own |
| **415** | God of grace and God of glory |
| **423** | Lord, whose love in humble service |
| **492** | O Master, let me walk with you |
| **510** | O God of youth, whose Spirit in our hearts is stirring |

## SHARING

| | |
|---|---|
| **409** | Praise and thanksgiving |

## SHEPHERD

| | |
|---|---|
| **336** | Jesus, thy boundless love to me |
| **371** | With God as our friend |
| **451** | The Lord's my shepherd |
| **456** | The King of love, my shepherd is |
| **481** | Savior, like a shepherd lead us |
| **501** | He leadeth me: oh, blessed thought |

## SICKNESS

See Healing

## SIN, CONFESSION OF

See Repentance, Forgiveness

## SOCIETY

See 413-437

| | |
|---|---|
| **122** | Love consecrates the humblest act |
| **126** | Where charity and love prevail |
| **140** | With high delight let us unite |
| **160** | Filled with the Spirit's pow'r with one accord |
| **233** | Thy strong word did cleave the darkness |
| **269** | Awake, my soul, and with the sun |
| **359** | In Christ there is no east or west |
| **363** | Christ is alive! Let Christians sing |
| **364** | Son of God, eternal Savior |
| **372** | In Adam we have all been one |

**SOCIETY** (continued)

| | |
|---|---|
| 373 | Eternal Ruler of the ceaseless round |
| 396 | O God, O Lord of heav'n and earth |
| 401 | Before you, Lord we bow |
| 462 | God the omnipotent! King who ordainest |
| 463 | God, who stretched the spangled heavens |
| 466 | Great God, our source and Lord of space |
| 493 | Hope of the world, thou Christ of great compassion |

**SOCIAL JUSTICE**

See Society

**SONG OF THE THREE YOUNG MEN**

| | |
|---|---|
| Cant. 18 | All you works of the Lord |
| 527 | All creatures of our God and King |

**SORROW**

| | |
|---|---|
| 106 | In the hour of trial |
| 295 | Out of the depths I cry to you |
| 319 | Oh, sing, my soul, your maker's praise |
| 453 | If you but trust in God to guide you |
| 454 | If God himself be for me |

See Comfort and Rest

**STEWARDSHIP**

See 404-412

| | |
|---|---|
| 362 | We plow the fields and scatter |
| 364 | Son of God, eternal Savior |
| 392 | O Lord, send forth your Spirit |
| 397 | O Zion, haste, your mission high fulfilling |
| 418 | Judge eternal, throned in splendor |
| 424 | Lord of glory, you have bought us |
| 425 | O God of mercy, God of light |
| 447 | All depends on our possessing |
| 548 | Oh, worship the King, all-glorious above |
| 563 | For the fruit of all creation |

## SUNDAY

| | |
|---|---|
| 246 | The first day of the week |
| 251 | O day of rest and gladness |
| | See *Easter; Beginning of Service* |

## TEACHERS

See *Education; Commitment*

## TE DEUM

| | |
|---|---|
| p. 139 | You are God, we praise you (in Morning prayer) |
| Cant. 3 | You are God, we praise you |
| 535 | Holy God, we praise your name |
| 547 | Thee we adore, eternal Lord |

## TEMPTATION

| | |
|---|---|
| 106 | In the hour of trial |
| 343 | Guide me ever, great Redeemer |
| 439 | What a friend we have in Jesus |
| 450 | Who trusts in God, a strong abode |
| 453 | If you but trust in God to guide you |
| 503 | O Jesus, I have promised |

## THANKSGIVING, DAY OF

| | |
|---|---|
| 241 | We praise you, O God, our redeemer, creator |
| 264 | When all your mercies, O my God |
| 362 | We plow the fields and scatter |
| 404 | As saints of old their firstfruits brought |
| 407 | Come, you thankful people, come |
| 409 | Praise and thanksgiving |
| 412 | Sing to the Lord of harvest |
| 437 | Not alone for mighty empire |
| 465 | Evening and morning |
| 527 | All creatures of our God and King |
| 533, 534 | Now thank we all our God |
| 543 | Praise to the Lord, the Almighty, the King of creation! |
| 557 | Let all things now living |
| 560 | Oh, that I had a thousand voices |
| 561 | For the beauty of the earth |
| 563 | For the fruit of all creation |

## TRANSFIGURATION OF OUR LORD

| | |
|---|---|
| 76 | O Morning Star, how fair and bright |
| 80 | Oh, wondrous type! Oh, vision fair |
| 89 | How good, Lord to be here! |
| 265 | Christ, whose glory fills the skies |
| 511 | Renew me, O eternal Light |
| 518 | Beautiful Savior |
| 526 | Immortal, invisible, God only wise |
| 536 | O God of God, O Light of Light |

## TRAVELERS

| | |
|---|---|
| 467 | Eternal Father, strong to save |
| | See Pilgrimage |

## TRIAL

See Comfort and Rest; Sorrow; Temptation

## TRINITY

See Holy Trinity

## TRUST, GUIDANCE

See 445-485

| | |
|---|---|
| 77 | O one with God the Father |
| 102 | On my heart imprint your image |
| 104 | In the cross of Christ I glory |
| 107 | Beneath the cross of Jesus |
| 188 | I bind unto myself today |
| 248 | Dearest Jesus, at your word |
| 270 | God of our life, all-glorious Lord |
| 293, 294 | My hope is built on nothing less |
| 295 | Out of the depths I cry to you |
| 305 | I lay my sins on Jesus |
| 319 | Oh, sing, my soul, your maker's praise |
| 320 | O God, our help in ages past |
| 325 | Lord, thee I love with all my heart |
| 326 | My heart is longing to praise my Savior |
| 333 | Lord, take my hand and lead me |
| 334 | Jesus, Savior, pilot me |
| 341 | Jesus, still lead on |
| 343 | Guide me ever, great Redeemer |

**TRUST GUIDANCE (continued)**

| | |
|---|---|
| 361 | Do not despair, O little flock |
| 366 | Lord of our life and God of our salvation |
| 395 | I trust, O Christ, in you alone |
| 399 | We are the Lord's. His all-sufficient merit |
| 441 | Eternal Spirit of the living Christ |
| 444 | With the Lord begin your task |
| 460 | I am trusting you, Lord Jesus |
| 494 | Jesus calls us; o'er the tumult |
| 495 | Lead on, O King eternal! |
| 501 | He leadeth me: oh, blessed thought! |
| 507 | How firm a foundation, O saints of the Lord |
| 539 | Praise the Almighty, my soul, adore him |
| 552 | In thee is gladness |
| 562 | Lift ev'ry voice and sing! |

**VISITATION**

| | |
|---|---|
| 86 | The only Son from heaven |

**WATCHFULNESS**

| | |
|---|---|
| 31 | Wake, awake, for night is flying |
| 269 | Awake, my soul, and with the sun |
| 383 | Rise up, O saints of God! |
| 443 | Rise, my soul, to watch and pray |
| 480 | Oh, that the Lord would guide my ways |

**WARFARE, CHRISTIAN**

| | |
|---|---|
| 177, 178 | By all your saints in warfare |
| 183 | The Son of God goes forth to war |
| 389 | Stand up, stand up for Jesus |
| 399 | We are the Lord's. His all-sufficient merit! |
| 461 | Fight the good fight with all your might |
| 495 | Lead on, O King eternal! |
| 509 | Onward, Christian soldiers |

**WEDDING**

| | |
|---|---|
| Cant. 16 | I will sing the story of your love, O Lord |
| 76 | O Morning Star, how fair and bright! |
| 78 | All praise to you, O Lord |
| 287 | O perfect Love, all human thought transcending |
| 288 | Hear us now, our God and Father |

## WEDDING (continued)

| | |
|---|---|
| 289 | Heav'nly Father, hear our prayer |
| 315 | Love divine, all loves excelling |
| 354 | Eternal God, before your throne we bend |
| 481 | Savior, like a shepherd lead us |
| 487 | Let us ever walk with Jesus |
| 512 | Oh, blest the house, whate'er befall |
| 513 | Come, my way, my truth, my life |
| 518 | Beautiful Savior |
| 533, 534 | Now thank we all our God |
| 551 | Joyful, joyful we adore thee |
| 552 | In thee is gladness |

## WITNESS

*See 376-403*

| | |
|---|---|
| 156 | Look, oh, look, the sight is glorious |
| 160 | Filled with the Spirit's pow'r, with one accord |
| 161 | O day full of grace that now we see |
| 170 | Crown him with many crowns |
| 179 | At the name of Jesus |
| 218 | Strengthen for service, Lord, the hands |
| 230 | Lord, keep us steadfast in your Word |
| 231 | O Word of God incarnate |
| 234 | Almighty God, your Word is cast |
| 242 | Let the whole creation cry |
| 252 | You servants of God, your master proclaim |
| 283 | O God, send heralds who will never falter |
| 285 | Spirit of God, sent from heaven abroad |
| 355 | Through the night of doubt and sorrow |
| 372 | In Adam we have all been one |
| 374 | We all believe in one true God |
| 379 | Spread, oh, spread, almighty Word |
| 433 | The Church of Christ, in ev'ry age |
| 434 | The Son of God, our Christ, the Word, the Way |
| 462 | God the omnipotent! King who ordainest |
| 523 | Holy Spirit, ever dwelling |
| 530 | Jesus shall reign where'er the sun |
| 556 | Herald, sound the note of judgment |
| 559 | Oh, for a thousand tongues to sing |

*See Word, The*

## WORD, THE

See 227-240
**250** Open now thy gates of beauty
See Scriptures

## WORK, DAILY

**269** Awake, my soul, and with the sun
**404** As saints of old their first fruits brought
**436** All who love and serve your city
**444** With the Lord begin your task
**465** Evening and morning
**469** Lord of all hopefulness, Lord of all joy
**504** O God, my faithful God
**505** Forth in thy name, O Lord, I go
See Society

## WORLD

See Creation; Society

## WORSHIP

**187** Dearest Jesus, we are here
**245** All people that on earth do dwell
**247** Holy Majesty, before you
**249** God himself is present
**375** Only-begotten, Word of God eternal
**391** And have the bright immensities
**465** Evening and morning
**514** O Savior, precious Savior
**548** Oh, worship the King, all-glorious above
**555** When in our music God is glorified

## ZEAL

**37** Hark! A thrilling voice is sounding
**269** Awake, my soul, and with the sun